Quilts of Thimble Creek

PRODUCED BY KOOLER DESIGN STUDIO, INC

10 9 8 7 6 5 4 3 2

Library of Congress Cataloging-in-Publication Data

Kooler, Donna

Quilts of ThimbleCreek

"A Leisure Arts Publication"

ISBN: 1-57486-285-5

Contributors

Project Designers
Alex Anderson
Sue Falkowski
Joanna Figueroa
Marg Gair
Donna Heppler
Sandy Klop
Lori Le Var
Verna Mosquera
Lisa Quan
Sandy Newman
Laura Nownes
Lisa Stone
Joe Wood
Roxie Wood

If you have questions or comments please contact:

Leisure Arts Customer Service
P.O. Box 55595
Little Rock, AR 72215-9633
www.leisurearts.com

Kooler Design Studio, Inc.
399 Taylor Blvd., Suite 104
Pleasant Hill, CA 94523
kds@koolerdesign.com

ThimbleCreek Quilt Shop
1536 Newell Avenue
Walnut Creek, CA 94596
925-946-9970
www.thimblecreek.com

Published by
LEISURE ARTS

Creative Director
Donna Kooler

Editor in Chief
Judy Swager

Editor
Jo Lynn Taylor

Book Design & Production
Nancy Wong Spindler

Writers
Store: Kit Schlich
Introductions: Sudha Putnam

Text Editor
Sudha Putnam

Copy Editor/Index
Joan Cravens

Illustrations
Jo Lynn Taylor

Proofreaders
Sandy Orton, Priscilla Timm

Photography/Color Separator
Dianne Woods, Berkeley, CA

Photo Stylist
Basha Hanner

Produced by

Table of Contents

ThimbleCreek: A Quilter's Paradise

Come with us to visit ThimbleCreek, a remarkable shop that caters to the desires of a thriving community of quilting enthusiasts. You'll find it nestled in downtown Walnut Creek, California, part of the greater San Francisco Bay Area. Under the care of owners Roxie and Joe Wood, ThimbleCreek is a meeting place where shoppers can hang out and feel at home. A comfy couch encourages lounging and perusing books and magazines. Aisles of fabric—estimated at as many as 8,000 bolts!—invite customers to browse among their favorite color pathways. A rustic farm cart practically bursts with bundles of fat quarters, that spill over into wicker baskets and farm pails, lending a delightful informality.

At the heart of the store is a massive cutting table graced with fresh flowers and the buzz of creative energy as quilters plan out their new projects and make final fabric selections. The shop's high ceilings provide ample gallery space for display of approximately 100 quilts at a time. But perhaps ThimbleCreek's greatest treasure is the knowledgeable staff that is integral to the store's success. Quilters and crafters themselves, many of the same employees cutting your fabric also teach ThimbleCreek's legendary classes.

Opening its doors in 1994, ThimbleCreek now boasts 6000 square feet, including two full-size classrooms and additional work space "as needed." In short, ThimbleCreek has everything a beginner or an advanced quilter needs and desires.

Pursuing a Dream

A shop as successful as ThimbleCreek doesn't happen by accident. It arose from a small nucleus of individuals who were able to use their quilting enthusiasm and expertise to forge a creative yet realistic retail plan.

Our story begins with Roxie Wood, who loved to sew. With several friends, Roxie sponsored craft boutiques in her home twice a year, displaying tables full of their handwork to the public. Later, she worked in a local quilting shop. Her experience of manning a vendor's booth at a local quilt show led her to consider opening her own quilting shop. It was obvious that quilts were her favorite thing to design and sell.

Roxie and her first partner, Janey Edwards, spied an empty store front in a small strip mall awaiting a new tenant and fell in love with the 4000-square-foot space. Viewing its large windows, high ceilings, and feeling of openness, they realized it would be just right for the shop they envisioned. They were poised to take the plunge, and with her husband, Joe, signed a second mortgage on their home to capitalize the fledgling enterprise.

To fill the space that initially looked so cavernous to the new retailers, Roxie and Janey cut and bundled a heap of fat quarters from their early fabric inventory to give the appearance of more fabric. It wasn't long, however, before the store offered ever-newer and more diverse merchandise for quilters. Roxie and Janey turned out to be a savvy buyers, and fabric simply flew off the shelves.

The Dream Realized

As ThimbleCreek continued to grow (adding 2000 more square feet initially used as a quilt gallery) the shop became an anchor for the small shops around it, rejuvenating the entire retail area. In 2000, Janey left the business to pursue other interests.

Joe Wood, Roxie's husband, had pursued art and business majors in college—a serendipitous blend, as it turns out. Retired from banking, Joe supports Roxie's vision for the store. He's even taken up quilting, and designed one of the quilts in this book. He still considers himself "Roxie's apprentice," but is a full-time business partner. He manages the ever-changing Web site (www.thimblecreek.com) which features the class schedule, shop news, sales, and special offers.

You can find Roxie and Joe in the shop nearly every day. Joe notes, "We work hard but we're having fun at it." Together they select most of the fabrics and maintain a sharp eye for what will be popular with their customers. Currently, that would be reproductions of old fabrics from as early as the Civil War era (1860s) to the 1930s, as well as plaids and flannels. The Woods carefully follow the trends of the quilt world and industry innovations. They recognize that quilters in their area have sophisticated tastes, read about all the current trends, and will ask for specific new fabrics. To that end, the Woods attend the quilt market shows twice a year and meet with all major fabric representatives four times a year. When not in the store, Joe attends the California School of Professional Fabric Design in Berkeley, with the dream of designing a ThimbleCreek line of fabrics with Roxie.

A Class for Everyone

The Woods' quest is to keep quilting "interesting, fresh, and new" for their customers, and they are as close to realizing this vision as any retailers can be. Above all, they've never wavered from their goal of fully serving their quilting community. Aside from offering great inventory, education is ThimbleCreek's greatest contribution. Recognizing that informed and skilled quilters make the best customers, the Woods offer a slate of classes that is remarkable both for the number of classes as well as the breadth of subject.

Three times a year Roxie devises a schedule of 130–170 classes. She's sure to poll her employees, who know first-hand what subjects the customers are interested in. The class mailing list goes off to about 13,000 people. Students range in age from six to 90, including a few men, one of whom made a quilt for his grandchildren.

Roxie must also select at least 80 teachers every four months. Many are plucked from the East Bay's impressive community of quilt experts. Others are ThimbleCreek employees; some are out-of-state quilt masters.

For each class, ThimbleCreek assigns a level of expertise required: one thimble icon for beginner, two for intermediate, and three for advanced. For the beginner, there are basic technique classes; often 30–40 names fill the waiting list. On the other end of the creative spectrum, there are classes for those interested in exploring the cutting edge of quilt innovation. In between are an array of classes featuring traditional quilts or some of the hottest new quilt styles made from specialty fabrics such as flannel and 1930s prints. Add a host of non-quilt projects that only ask that you know how to sew.

ThimbleCreek classes fall into several categories: Beginning Quilting, Quilts and Wallhangings (by far the largest category), Technique Workshops (including hand- and machine-quilting, photo transferring, piecing, appliqué, foundation piecing, redwork, silk ribbon embroidery, and more), Clothing Classes, Craft and Gift Ideas, and Dolls and Stuffed Animals. Here's a random sampling of what the Fall schedule offers: "American Spirit," a patriotic wallhanging by Sue Sprago; "Celebrations of Life," taught by Mary Lou Weidman and based on her book *Quilted Memories/Celebrations of Life*; "Free Form Machine Quilting Designs" by Kathy Sandbach; "Freddy's Playhouse," a bright, original quilt of houses, trees, and gardens taught by its designer, Freddy Moran; "Still Life," featuring appliqué and piecing, by Gerry Kimball-Carr; "Floral Impressions Using Foundation Piecing Stitch and Flip" by Jean Wells; and a huge array of winter holiday projects. An authors' book signing and trunk show support the publication of the book *Q is for Quilt* by Laura Nownes and Diana McClun.

Roxie's most recent brainstorm is "Quilting with Friends," a four-day quilting retreat held in Pacific Grove, a picturesque town on the Monterey peninsula, about a two-hour drive from Walnut Creek. It's just far enough to "get away from it all" without travel time eating up too much quilting time!

From ThimbleCreek to You...

It's clear that the secret of ThimbleCreek's success lies in the fact that the Woods and their employees have tapped into a vital and enthusiastic quilting community. And it's only natural that such creative energy should be shared with quilters outside the Bay Area. This book is ThimbleCreek's gift to the large community of world quilters. All the quilts in this book were designed by ThimbleCreek teachers and employees, who are often one and the same. Roxie and Joe selected designs that had maximum visual impact and appeal for you, the reader. Enjoy looking through the pages, enjoy the actual piecing and quilting, and enjoy the whole adventure!

❖

Alex Anderson

My love affair with quiltmaking began in 1978, when I completed a Grandmother's Flower Garden quilt as part of my work towards a degree in art from San Francisco State University. Little did I know that quilting would become a lifelong passion. My emphasis in college was fiber and graphic design, which led me to a deep respect and admiration of Amish quilts. Their strong visual impact along with the sensitive intricacy of the quilting design became the starting point of my quilting. Over the years, my focus has been on understanding fabric relationships and developing an intense appreciation of traditional quilts and beautiful quilting surface design.

Over two decades later I am still in love with quilting and all that surrounds it. The creative aspect of making a quilt or watching someone unlock his or her own creative spirit is one of pure joy and excitement. The journey of quiltmaking has challenged me in other ways I never thought possible. From authoring books to hosting "Simply Quilts" on Home and Garden Television, quiltmaking has allowed me to stretch and grow beyond my wildest dreams.

My personal mission is to share my love of quilting with anyone who will listen. When teaching, my goal is to educate and encourage those interested in quilting as clearly and simply as possible. As for those who really aren't interested in the craft itself, I enjoy enlightening them about this art that has been handed down so carefully from generation to generation.

Do I have time to quilt? Of course. It is the place I find myself most at home, the place where I can reflect and think about things, and the place where my creative spirit soars. I can't imagine my life without quilts…nor do I intend to.

Simply Beautiful

Designed and made by Alex Anderson; machine quilted by Paula Reid
Finished size: 60" x 60"

Many years ago I attended a trunk show of quilts presented by a nationally known teacher. *Exhilarating* couldn't begin to describe the experience. About halfway through the show, she gave a dissertation on the importance of collecting neutral fabrics. She presented the following case: Season to season a few spectacular neutrals will be introduced, but to obtain a healthy collection of neutrals, one must be on a constant search. She then posed the question, "Can anyone have too many neutrals?" The hunt was on! In time I found my stash filled with a wide variety of glorious neutrals. I discovered that this style of monochromatic coloration creates a beautiful, sophisticated, and subtle look.

When working in neutrals, even the simplest pattern stands out. The key to a successful neutral quilt is to use a large variety of fabrics with interesting prints. In addition, it is very important to use pure white. Without white, your quilt will look muddy and lack sparkle.

Materials

Yardage (based on 42" fabric, from selvage to selvage)

Fabric 1:	2½ yds. assorted whites and lights
Fabric 2:	2½ yds. assorted mediums and medium darks
Backing:	3½ yds.
Binding:	½ yd.
Batting:	65" x 65"

Sickle Block

(Fig. 1)

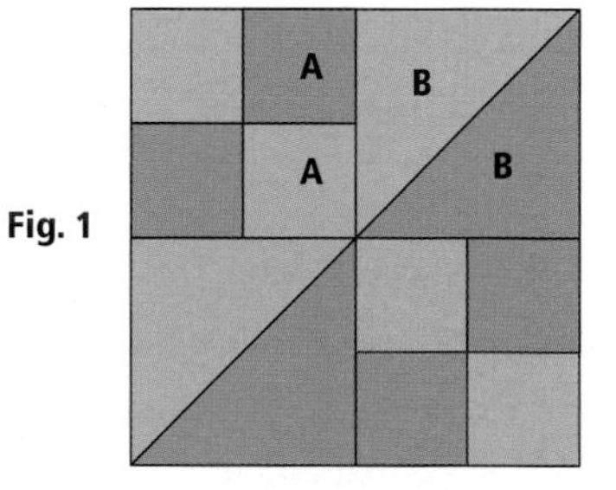

Fig. 1

Half-square Triangle Blocks

(Border, Fig. 2)

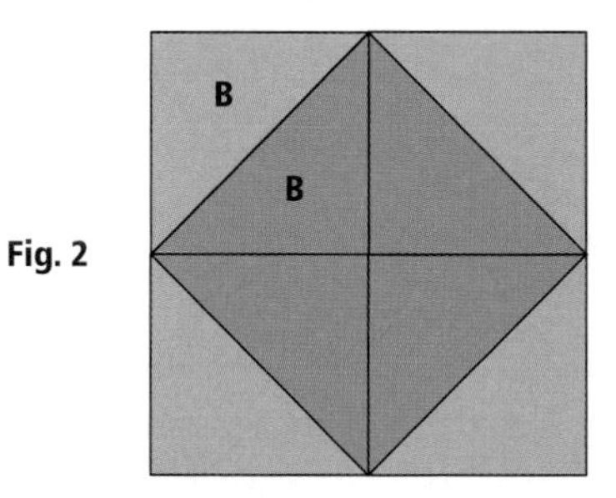

Fig. 2

Cutting

(See Quilt Layout Diagram)
Cut all fabric crosswise, from selvage to selvage unless otherwise instructed.

FABRIC 1

PIECE A: Cut (256) 2" squares.
PIECE B: Cut (64) 3⅞" squares, and then cut each square in half on the diagonal to create two triangles.

FABRIC 2

PIECE A: Cut (256) 2" squares.
PIECE B: Cut (64) 3⅞" squares, and then cut each square in half on the diagonal to create two triangles.

FABRIC 1

PIECE B: Cut (72) 3⅞" squares, and then cut each square in half on the diagonal to create two triangles.

FABRIC 2

PIECE B: Cut (72) 3⅞" squares, and then cut each square in half on the diagonal to create two triangles.

Simply Beautiful Quilt Layout

Fabric 1 - assorted white to light

Fabric 2 - assorted medium to medium-dark

Construction

Sew ¼" seams with right sides together unless otherwise noted.

Sickle Block

Finished size: 6" x 6"
(Make 64 blocks. See Fig. 1.)

To create each sickle block:

1. For each four-square unit, sew together a light square (A) and a dark square (A), and then press toward the dark square (Fig. 3). Repeat to create another A/A unit. Sew together the two A/A units, and then press toward the top unit. Repeat this step to create a total of two four-square units per block.

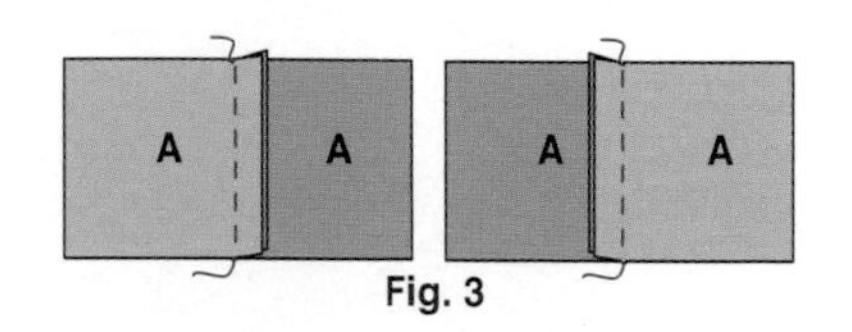

Fig. 3

2. Sew together a light triangle (B) and a dark triangle (B) to create a square. Press toward the dark triangle (Fig. 4). Repeat this step to create a total of two B/B units per block.

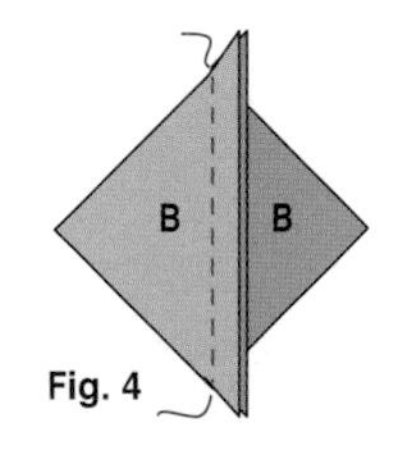

Fig. 4

3. Sew a four-square (A) unit to the left edge of a (B) unit, being sure that the upper-right square of the four-square unit is dark and the left edge of the B unit is light (Fig. 5). Press toward the four-square unit. Repeat this step, but this time sew the four-square (A) unit to the right of a B unit, being sure that the B edge is dark. Sew together the two rows and press toward the top row to complete the sickle block.

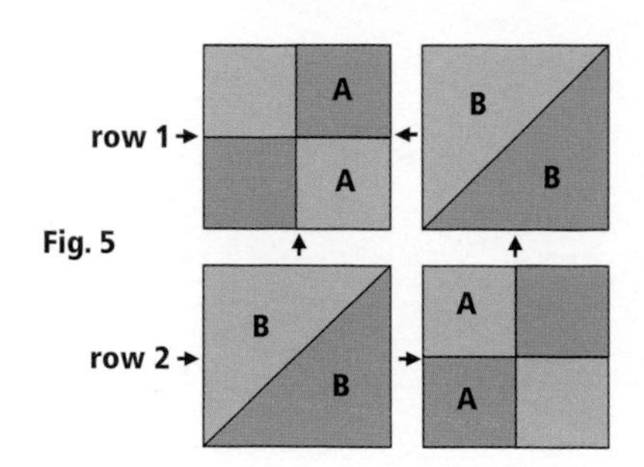

Fig. 5

Half-square Triangle Blocks

Finished size: 6" x 6"
(See Fig. 2. Make 36 blocks.)

To create each half-square triangle block:

1. Sew four light triangles (B) to four dark triangles (B). Press half the resulting units with the seams going toward the dark triangle, and press half with the seams going toward the light triangle. **Note:** While the pressing instructions for these blocks seems tricky, in the end they will help with ease of construction.

2. Arrange the B/B units as shown (Fig. 6), being sure that the pressing direction of each unit is as indicated. Half of your finished blocks should have a light center and half should have a dark center.

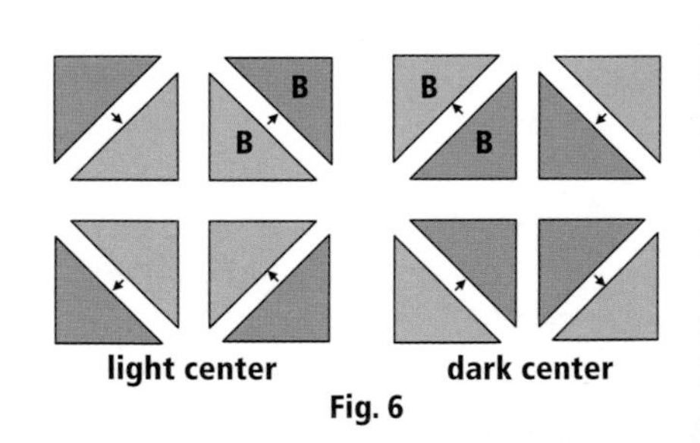

Fig. 6

3. Sew together the units, and then press the seams in the direction indicated (Fig. 7).

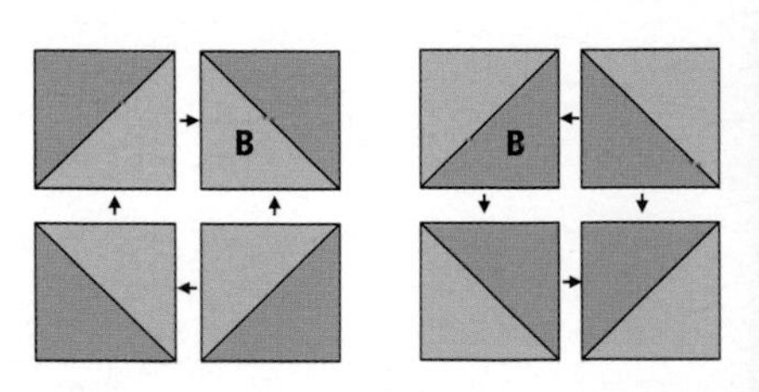

Fig. 7

Simply Beautiful by Alex Anderson

Assembly

1. Lay out the sickle blocks in eight rows of eight blocks each (Fig. 8).

2. Sew together the blocks in each row. Press each row of blocks in the opposite direction.

3. Sew together the eight finished rows and press.

4. To create the top and bottom borders, sew two rows of eight half-square triangle centered blocks (Fig. 9), alternating light and dark blocks. Sew one of these rows to the top, beginning with a dark centered block, and sew the second row to the bottom, beginning with a light centered block. Press.

5. To create the side borders, sew two rows of ten half-square triangle blocks, alternating light and dark blocks. Sew these rows to each side of the quilt, beginning with a light centered block on the left side and beginning with a dark centered block on the right side. Press and square quilt top.

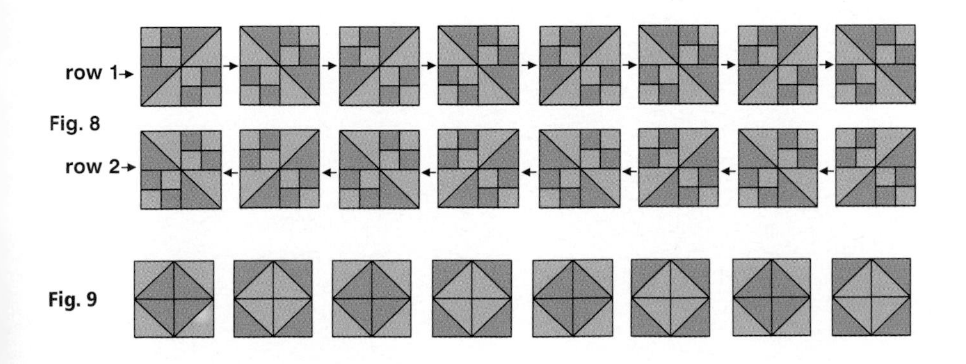

Quilting and Finishing

(See General Instructions pages 137–141)

1. Layer and baste together the quilt top, batting, and backing in preparation for quilting.

2. Hand or machine quilt. This quilt was machine-quilted with a triple cable stitch on the border, and a 2" cross-hatch grid for the interior.

3. Finish the quilt by cutting and piecing 2¼" strips of straight-grain binding fabric. Sew binding around the quilt using folded mitered corners. ❖

Garden Nine Patch

Designed and made by Alex Anderson; machine quilted by Paula Reid
Finished size: 53" x 60"

This quilt was inspired by an antique garden appliquéd quilt that was set on point with alternate nine patches. The quilt was incredibly appealing, yet I lacked the desire to appliqué all the alternate floral blocks. This large-scale floral decorator print, which I discovered in my collection, presented an easy solution. The only tricky part was to "fussy-cut" to maximize the large flowers in the print. The nine patches were a snap. Note that the dominant colors in the nine patches vary, and the appliquéd border uses several different greens, both in the vine and the leaves. The outside border is simply a repeat of the fabrics and colors used in the nine patch squares. This is an excellent quilt project for anyone who wants to celebrate his or her healthy fabric collection.

Materials

Yardage (based on 42" fabric, from selvage to selvage)

Fabric 1: 1 yd. large floral print
Fabric 2: 1½ yds. assorted light and dark
Fabric 3: 4 yds. white
Fabric 4: 1 yd. assorted greens
Backing: 4 yds.
Batting: 4 yds.
Binding: ½ yd.
¼" bias bar

Cutting

(See Quilt Layout Diagram)
Cut all fabric crosswise, from selvage to selvage, unless otherwise instructed.

Floral Blocks

FABRIC 1

PIECE A: Fussy-cut (30) 5" squares so large flowers of the fabric print are centered (see General Instructions page 128).

Nine Patch Blocks

(Fig. 1)

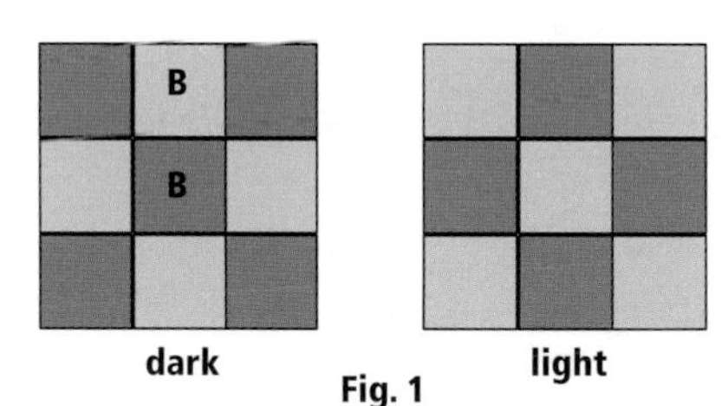

Fig. 1

FABRIC 2

PIECE B: Cut (378) 2" squares from the assorted darks and lights, keeping all lights and darks the same within a nine patch block.

FABRIC 3

PIECE C: Cut six 7⅝" squares, and then cut each square into quarters on both diagonals to create a total of 24 triangles. (You need only 22 triangles; you can discard two.)

PIECE D: Cut two 4" squares, and then cut each square in half on the diagonal to create the corner triangles.

Garden Nine-Patch Quilt Layout

Square-on-point Border

FABRIC 2

PIECE F: Cut (106) 2" squares.

PIECE J: Use Template J to cut approximately 20 flower bud tips in assorted pinks or reds. (See General Instructions, **Applique Hand or Machine Method**, pages 134–135).

FABRIC 3

PIECE G: Cut (51) 3¼" squares, then cut each square in quarters on the diagonal to create 204 side triangles.

PIECE H: Cut two 3" squares, then cut each square in half on the diagonal to create four corner triangles.

Vines

FABRIC 4

PIECE L: Cut 5⅝ yds. of 1" strips on the bias.

PIECE I: Use Template I to cut 45–50 leaves.

PIECE K: Use Template K to cut approximately 20 flower bud bases.

Construction

Nine Patch

Sew ¼" seams with right sides together unless otherwise noted.
Finished size: 4½" x 4½"
(See Fig. 1. Make 42 blocks.)

To make each nine patch block:

1. Sew nine squares (B) together from the assorted fabrics, alternating dark and light squares within each block (Fig. 2). Press the light seams toward dark seams. You will have a random amount of dark and light blocks.

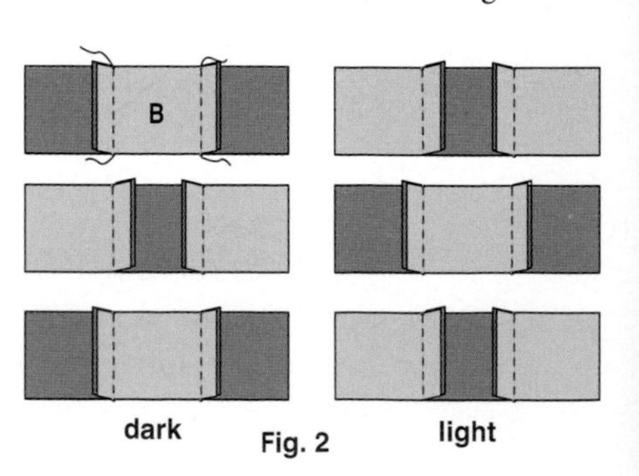

Fig. 2

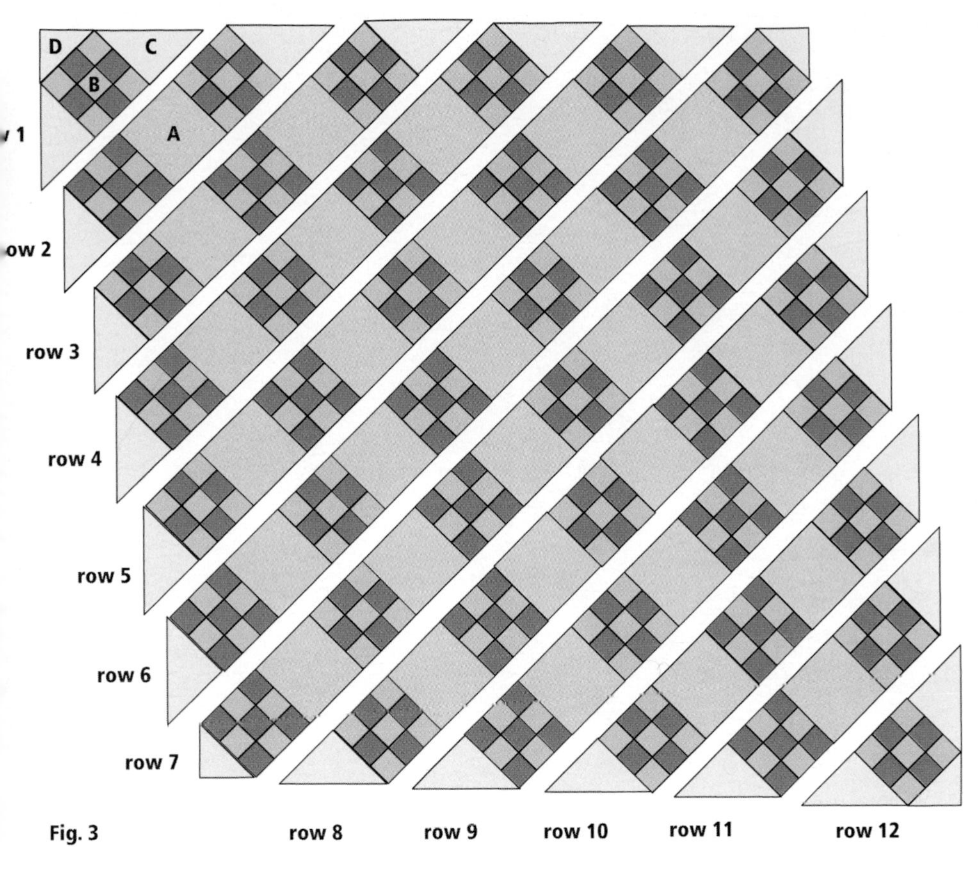

Fig. 3

Assembly
Quilt Top

To create the quilt top:

1. Lay out the nine patch and floral blocks in diagonal rows (A) in a pleasing arrangement, always starting with a nine patch.

2. Sew the blocks into rows, adding the corner (D) and side triangles (C) (Fig. 3) and press the seams of each row in opposite directions.

3. Sew the rows together. Press.

Outer Square-on-point Border
(Fig. 6)

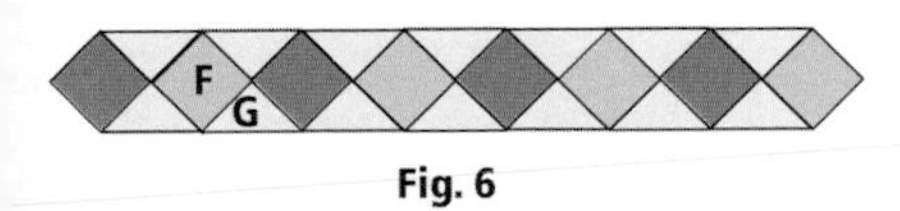

Fig. 6

1. To create each square-on-point unit, sew a triangle (G) to both sides of a square (F), making sure that the long side of one triangle faces up and the long side of the other triangle faces down (Fig. 7). Make a total of 98 units. Press the seams away from the square.

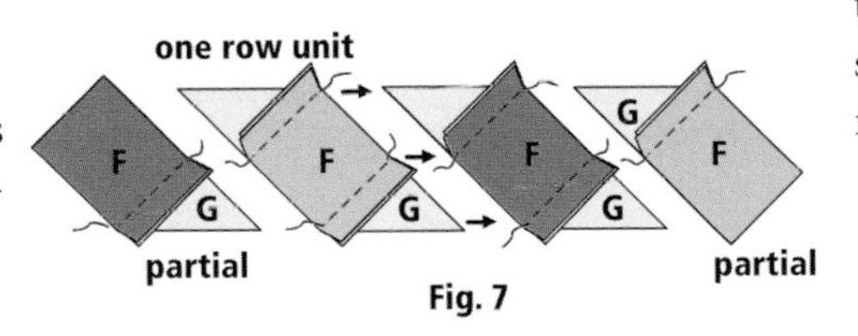

Fig. 7

2. Make 8 partial units by sewing one triangle (G) to one side of square (F) (Fig. 7–partial unit.)

3. For the top and bottom border, sew two rows of 23- full and 2 partial square-on-point units.

4. For the side borders, sew two sets of 26 full square-on-point and two partial units.

White Border

Your quilt should measure 38¾" x 45⅛". If it does, use the following measurements for the solid white border; if not, make the necessary width adjustments to the strips (E) (see General Instructions page 136).

1. Using Fabric 3, cut two 6⅞" x 45⅛" strips (E) lengthwise for the sides of the border. Sew a strip to each side of the quilt; press .

2. Using Fabric 3, cut two 6⅞" x 52" strips (E) lengthwise for the top and bottom of the border. Sew the strips to the top and bottom of the quilt and press and trim.

Appliqué Vine Border

To create the vine border:

1. To create the vine, sew together bias strips (L) end to end until you have created a 5½ yd. strip (Fig. 4).

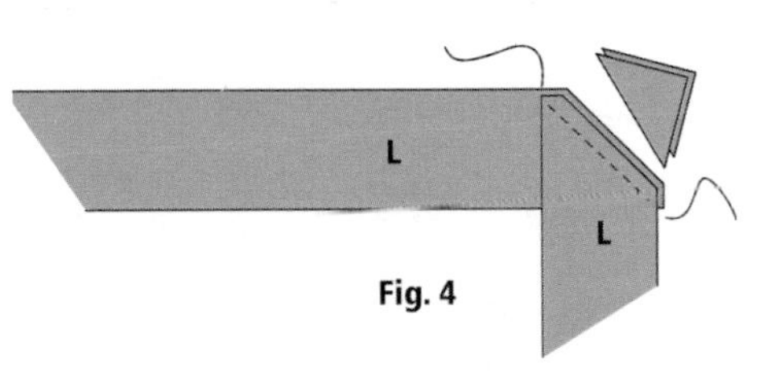

Fig. 4

2. Fold the fabric in half, right sides facing out, press, and sew a ¼" seam. Insert a ¼" bias bar into the resulting tube and gently roll and press the raw seams underneath. Remove the bias bar, being careful not to touch it as it may be hot. Trim any excess seam allowance that protrudes from underneath (Fig. 5).

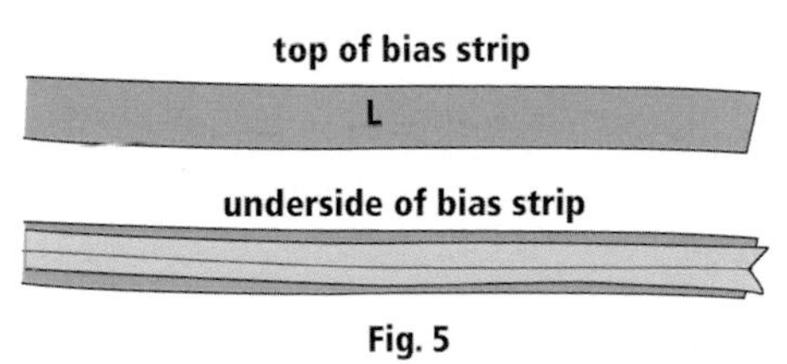

Fig. 5

3. Sew partial bud base (K) to bud tips (J), using your preferred appliqué technique (see General Instructions pages 134–135.)

4. Lay out the vine, leaves, and buds in a pleasing arrangement on the white border. Appliqué as desired.

5. Sew the pieced border rows to the top and bottom of the quilt and press.

Garden Nine Patch by Alex Anderson

6. Sew the pieced border rows to each side of the quilt, making sure that the squares meet up in the corners (Fig 8). Then sew squares together at corners; press.

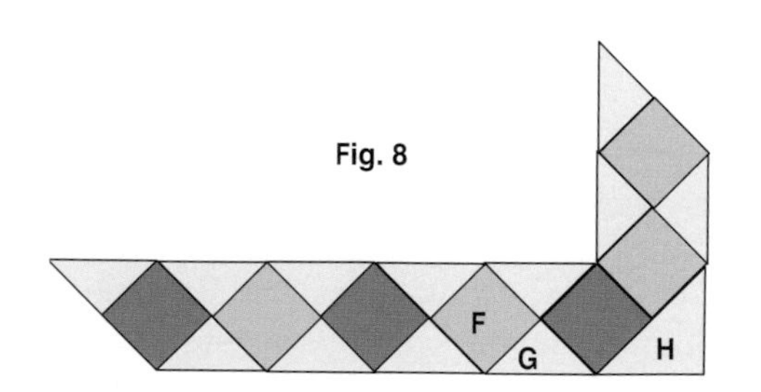

7. Sew a white triangle (H) to each corner to complete the quilt top.

Quilting and Finishing

(See General Instructions pages 137–141)

1. Layer and baste together the quilt top, batting, and backing in preparation for quilting.

2. Hand or machine quilt. For the interior of this quilt, I used a 1½" cross-hatch grid. For the appliqué and outside borders, I used a commercial cable-and-feather pattern.

3. Finish the quilt by cutting and piecing 2¼" strips of straight-grain binding fabric. Sew binding around the quilt using folded mitered corners. ❖

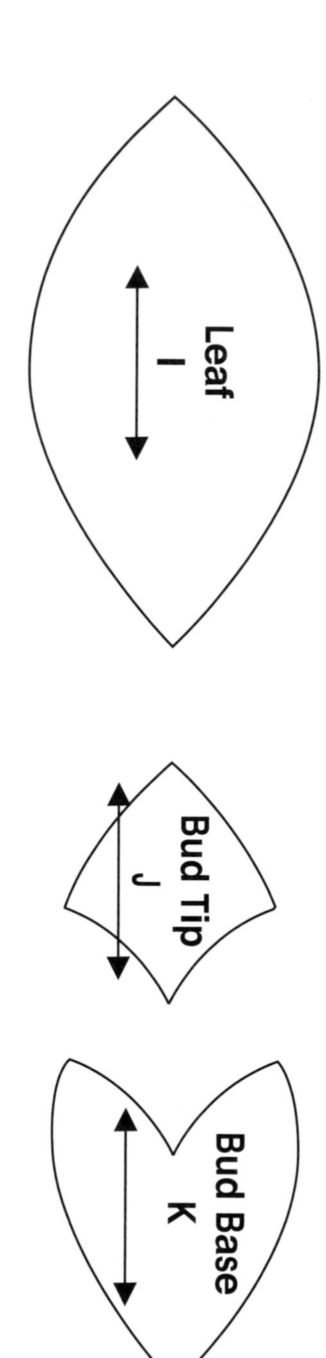

Sue Falkowski

I BEGAN QUILTING ABOUT FOUR YEARS AGO WHEN I HAD TO REPLACE A SEWING machine and learned about my great-grandmother and what a wonderful quilter and seamstress she was. She did quite a bit of embroidery, cutwork and redwork, and Sunbonnet Sue seems to have been among her favorites. Hearing about her work inspired me to enroll in a beginning quilting class at ThimbleCreek with my mom. We were quickly hooked and took as many classes as we could. We have had some great teachers. Seeing other quilter's work and their ideas is a constant source of inspiration. I like traditional designs and lately have been working with florals, hand-dyeing, and batiks. I love the watercolor effect.

Now, my sister and niece also enjoy quilting. I have a very understanding, patient "quilt husband," two wonderful daughters in college, and a teenage son who loves to play the drums and is learning to drive. Our unique little dog Shadow and a couple of parakeets keep me company as I quilt.

Someday I would like to live in the mountains. My favorite times were spent at my grandparent's cabin near Mt. Lassen. Nothing can fill the need for peace like time spent sitting outdoors, listening to the wind in the trees and enjoying the smell of pine. Quilting somehow comes close to that.

Asilomar Sunset

Designed, made, and quilted by Sue Falkowski
Finished size: 45" x 45"

Asilomar Sunset is the result of a class on color that I attended during a week-long seminar on quilting. The instructor had a wonderful way of encouraging students to experiment with colors to create unique patterns and designs. What makes this quilt special is the combination of colors in a rather simple block. The block is the same throughout, but the colors vary subtly between blocks. Although I used a variety of batiks, mottled, and tone-on-tone fabrics, they are all understated and not well-defined—more like washes. Batiks and hand-dyes are nice to work with because of the variation of light and dark and intensity between colors within a fabric. This gives a feeling of texture, richness, and softness. In this quilt I used two different batiks with common colors—peach with yellow and yellow with peach—to create the impression of overlap between blocks.

Materials

Yardage (based on 42" fabric, from selvage to selvage)

Fabric 1: 1 yd. large floral
Fabric 2: ½ yd. medium to dark red batik
Fabric 3: ½ yd. dark green batik
Fabric 4: ½ yd. light yellow batik
Fabric 5: ½ yd. peach batik
Fabric 6: ½ yd. total assorted greens
Fabric 7: ¼ yd. burgundy batik
Fabric 8: ¼ yd. total assorted lavender batiks
Fabric 9: ¼ yd. pale yellow
Fabric 10: ¼ yd. light coral batik
Fabric 11: ⅞ yd. floral print
Backing: 3 yds. pale rose floral
Binding: ½ yd.
Batting: 55" x 55" piece or twin size

Cutting

(See Quilt Layout Diagram)
Cut all fabric crosswise, from selvage to selvage, unless otherwise instructed.

Aunt Dinah Block

Make five of Variation 1; make four of Variation 2. (Fig. 1)

FABRIC 1

Piece A: Fussy-cut nine 3½" squares so large flowers of the fabric print are centered.

FABRIC 2

Piece B: Cut nine 4¼" squares, and then cut each square twice on the diagonal to create 36 triangles.

FABRIC 3

Piece C: Cut (18) 4¼" squares, and then cut each square twice on the diagonal to create 72 triangles.

FABRIC 4

Piece D: Variation 1 – Cut five 4¼" squares, and then cut each square twice on the diagonal to create 20 triangles .
Piece E: Variation 2 – Cut eight 3⅞" squares, and then cut each square once on the diagonal to create 16 triangles.

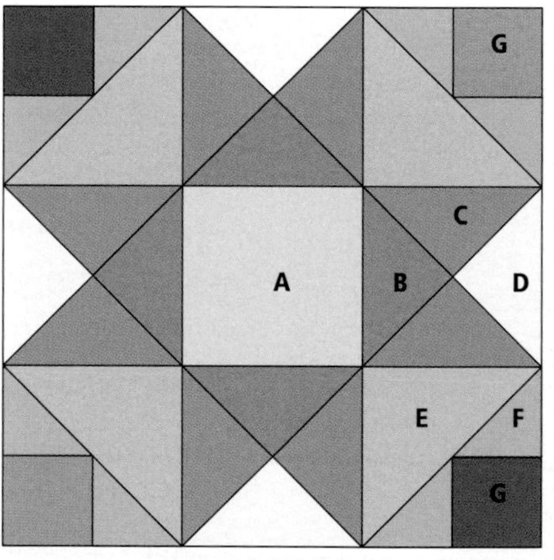

Fig. 1 - Variation 1

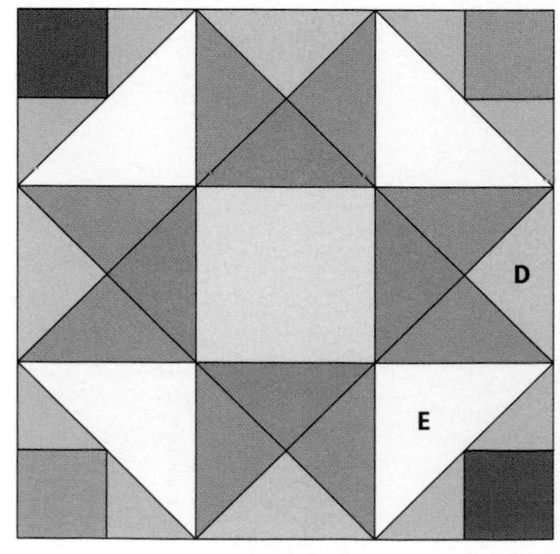

Fig. 1 - Variation 2

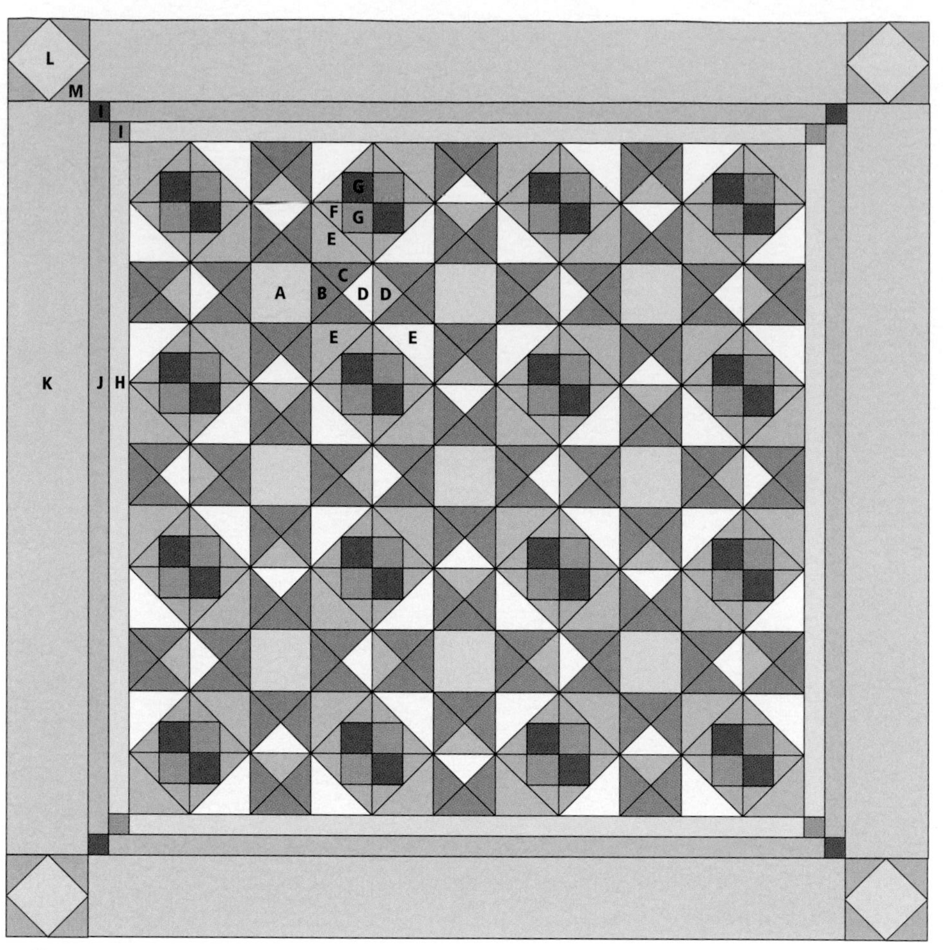

Asilomar Sunset Quilt Layout

- **Fabric 1 - large floral**
- **Fabric 2 – medium to dark red batik**
- **Fabric 3 – dark green batik**
- **Fabric 4 - light yellow batik**
- **Fabric 5 - peach batik**
- **Fabric 6 - assorted greens**
- **Fabric 7 - burgundy batik**
- **Fabric 8 – assorted lavender batiks**
- **Fabric 9 – pale yellow**
- **Fabric 10 - light coral batik**
- **Fabric 11 - floral print (third border)**

FABRIC 5

PIECE D: Variation 2 – Cut four 4¼" squares, and then cut each square twice on the diagonal to create 16 triangles.

PIECE E: Variation 1 – Cut ten 3⅞" squares, and then cut each square once on the diagonal to create 20 triangles.

FABRIC 6

PIECE F: Cut (36) 2⅜"squares, and then cut each square once on the diagonal to create 72 triangles.

FABRIC 7

PIECE G: Cut (18) 2" squares.

FABRIC 8

PIECE G: Cut (18) 2" squares.

Partial Blocks

Make 12 blocks: four of Variations 1 and 2; two of Variations 3 and 4. (Fig. 2)

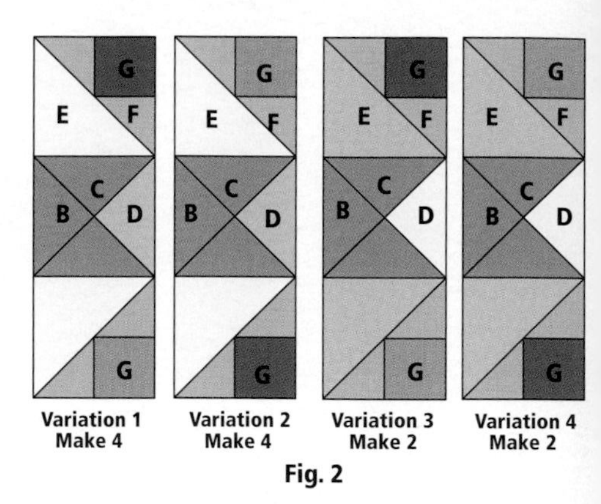

Fig. 2

FABRIC 2

PIECE B: Cut three 4¼" squares, and then cut each square twice on the diagonal to create 12 triangles.

FABRIC 3

PIECE C: Cut six 4¼" squares, and then cut each square twice on the diagonal to create 24 triangles.

FABRIC 4

PIECE D: Variations 3 and 4 – Cut one 4¼" square, and then cut the square twice on the diagonal to create four triangles.

PIECE E: Variations 1 and 2 – Cut eight 3⅞" squares, and then cut each square once on the diagonal to create 16 triangles.

FABRIC 5

PIECE D: Variations 1 and 2 – Cut two 4¼" squares, and then cut each square twice on the diagonal to create eight triangles.

PIECE E: Variations 3 and 4 – Cut four 3⅞" squares, and then cut each square once on the diagonal to create 8 triangles.

FABRIC 6

PIECE F: Cut (24) 2⅜" squares, and then cut each square once on the diagonal to create 48 triangles.

FABRIC 7

PIECE G: Cut (12) 2" squares.

FABRIC 8

PIECE G: Cut (12) 2" squares.

Asilomar Sunset by Sue Falkowski

Corner Blocks

Make four blocks: two of Variation 1 and two of Variation 2. (Fig. 3)

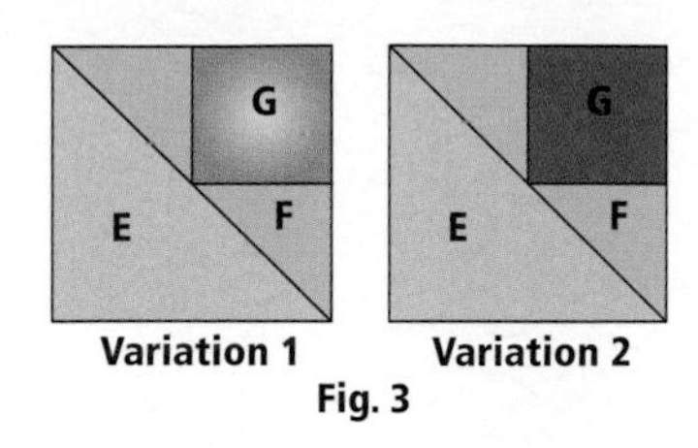

Fig. 3

FABRIC 6

PIECE F: Cut four 2⅜" squares, and then cut each square once on the diagonal to create 8 triangles.

FABRIC 7

PIECE G: Variation 2 – Cut two 2" squares.

FABRIC 8

PIECE G: Variation 1 – Cut two 2" squares.

First Border

(See Quilt Layout Diagram)

FABRIC 8

PIECE I: Cut four 1½" squares.

FABRIC 9

PIECE H: Cut four 1½" strips.

Second Border

(See Quilt Layout Diagram)

FABRIC 7

PIECE I: Cut four 1½" squares.

FABRIC 10

PIECE J: Cut four 1½" strips.

Third Border

(See Quilt Layout Diagram)

FABRIC 1

PIECE L: Fussy-cut four 3⅜" squares so large flowers of the fabric print are centered.

FABRIC 6

PIECE M: Cut eight 2⅞" squares, and then cut each square once on the diagonal to make 16 triangles.

FABRIC 11

PIECE K: Cut four 4½" strips.

Construction

Sew ¼" seams with right sides together unless otherwise noted.

Aunt Dinah Block

Finished size: 9" x 9"
(See Fig. 1. Make nine blocks: five of Variation 1; four of Variation 2.

To make each nine-patch Aunt Dinah block:

1. Select pieces for the block, alternating the fabric used in Piece D (Fabric 4 or 5) with the fabric used in Piece E, and using both Fabrics 7 and 8 for the small squares (G).

2. Sew together Pieces B and C, and then Pieces D and C. Press toward Piece C (Fig. 4). Then, sew together these units and press to create one patch. Repeat this step to create a total of four patches.

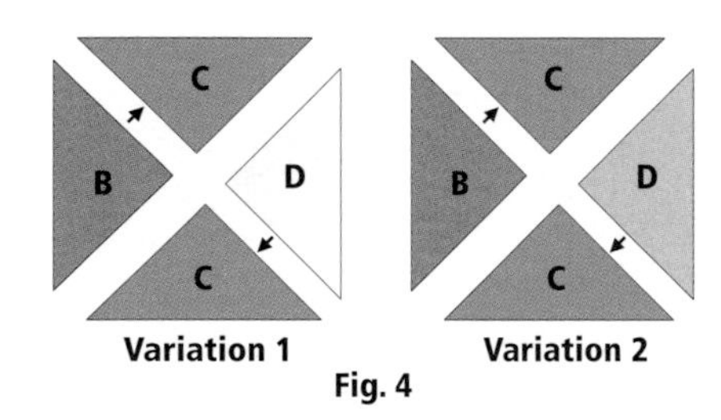

Fig. 4

3. Sew a small triangle (F) to a small square (G). Sew a second triangle (F) to the square (G). Press away from the square. Sew the unit to a large triangle (E) to create one patch (Fig. 5). Press toward the large triangle (E). Repeat this step to create a total of four patches, half with a burgundy square (G, Fabric 7) and half with a lavender square (G, Fabric 8).

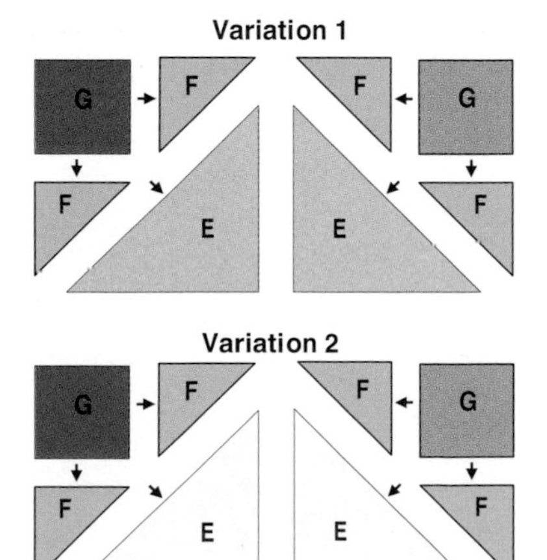

Fig. 5

4. Lay out the sewn patches and one floral patch (A) to create three rows of patches (Fig. 6). Be sure to alternate the color of the small squares (G). Sew together the patches in each row, pressing in opposite directions, and then sew the three rows together to complete the nine patch. Press.

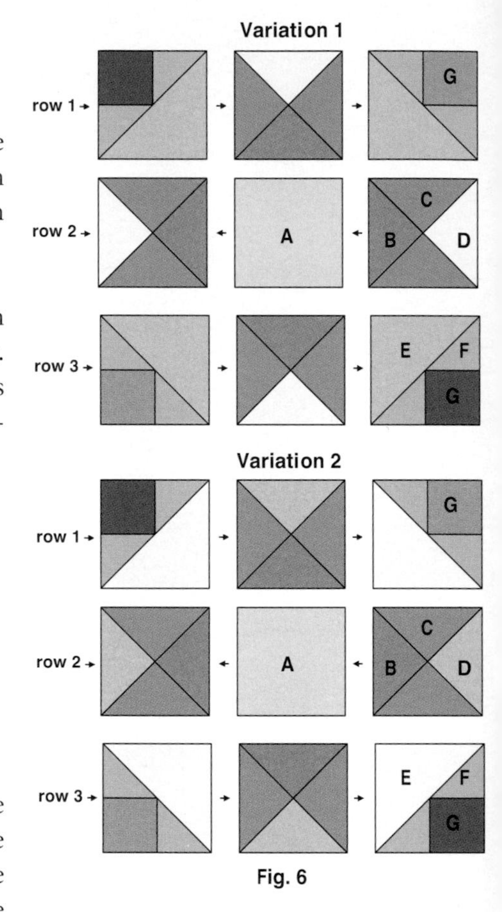

Fig. 6

Partial Block

Finished size: 3" x 9"
(See Fig. 2. Make 12 blocks.)

To make each partial block:

1. Select pieces for the block, alternating Fabrics 4 and 5 for Pieces D and E and Fabrics 7 and 8 for small squares (G).

2. Sew together Pieces B and C, and then Pieces D and C. Then, sew together these units to create one patch as done for the Aunt Dinah block (See Fig. 4).

3. Sew a small triangle (F) to a small square (G). Sew a second triangle (F) to the square (G). Sew the unit to a large triangle (E) to create one patch as done for the Aunt Dinah block (See Fig. 5). Repeat this step once.

4. Sew together the three patches to complete a partial block. Press each seam in opposite directions (Fig. 7).

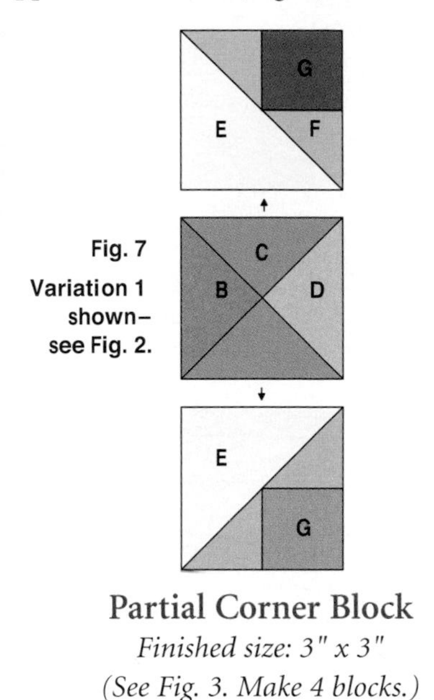

Partial Corner Block

Finished size: 3" x 3"

(See Fig. 3. Make 4 blocks.)

To make each corner block:
Sew a small triangle (F) to a small square (G). Sew a second triangle (F) to the square (G). Sew the unit to a large triangle (E) and press to complete the square as done for the Aunt Dinah block (See Fig. 5).

Assembly
Aunt Dinah Blocks

(Fig. 8)

1. Lay out Aunt Dinah, partial, and corner blocks, being sure to alternate color patterns (Variations 1 and 2). Sew together the blocks and partial blocks in rows, alternating the pressing direction. Sew together the rows to complete the quilt body.

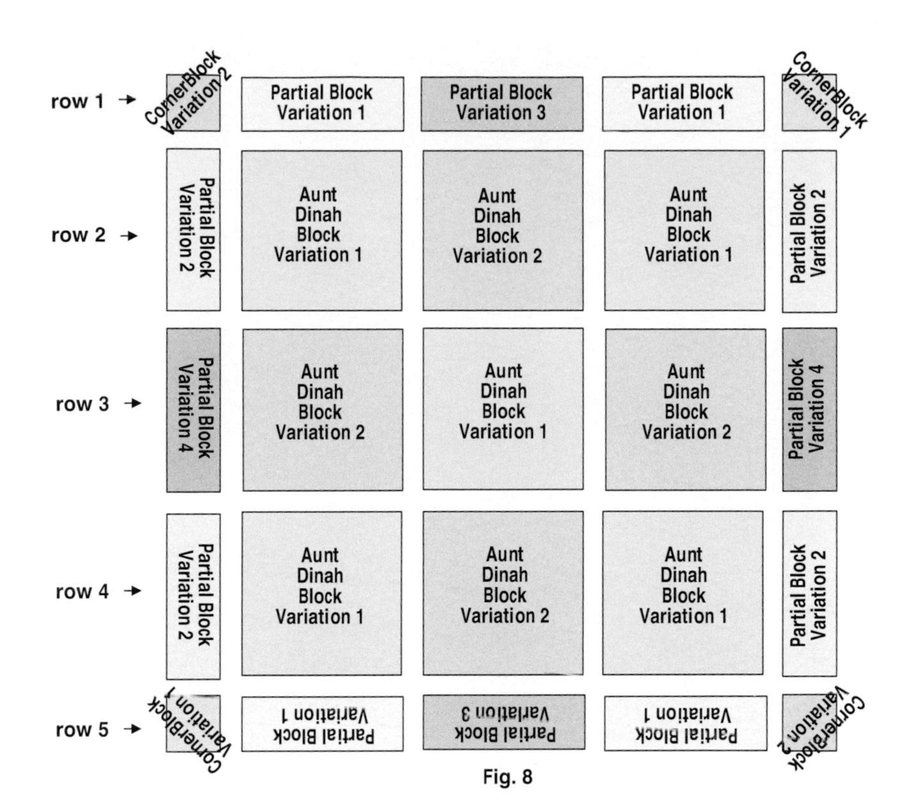

Fig. 8

Borders

(Fig. 9)

2. To create the first border, sew the border strip (H) to opposite sides of the quilt; press and trim to fit.

3. Measure across finished quilt top only (excluding side borders (H) for top and bottom border length. Add ½" to this measurement. Trim two strips (H) to this length. Sew a Fabric 8 square (I) to each end of the two strips; press.

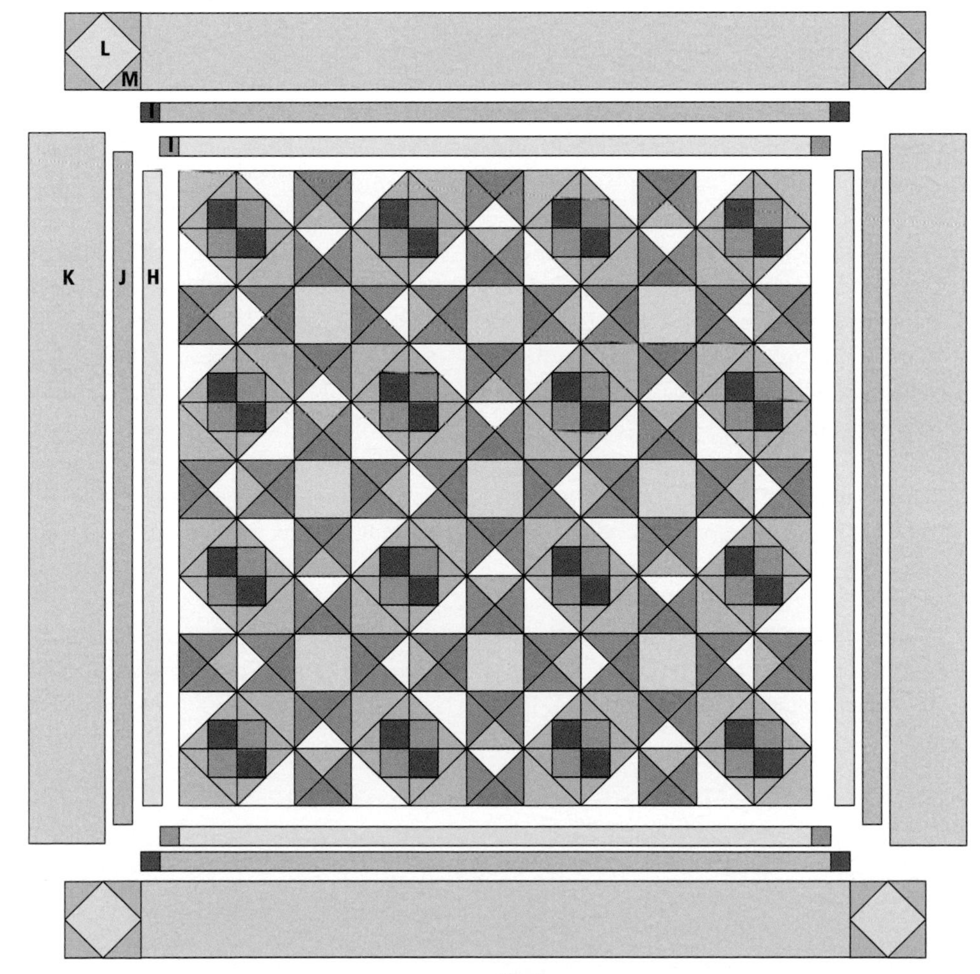

Fig. 9

4. Sew (H/I) strip units to the top and bottom of quilt.

5. To create the second border; sew a border strip (J) to opposite sides of the quilt; press and trim to fit.

6. Measure across finished quilt top including side borders (H) only, for top and bottom border length. Add ½" to this measurement. Trim two strips (J) to this length. Sew a Fabric 7 square (I) to each end of the two strips, press.

7. Sew (J/I) strip units to top and bottom of quilt; press.

8. For the third border, first make a Diamond in a Square by sewing a triangle (M) to each side of floral square (L). Repeat to create a total of four squares (Fig. 10).

Fig. 10

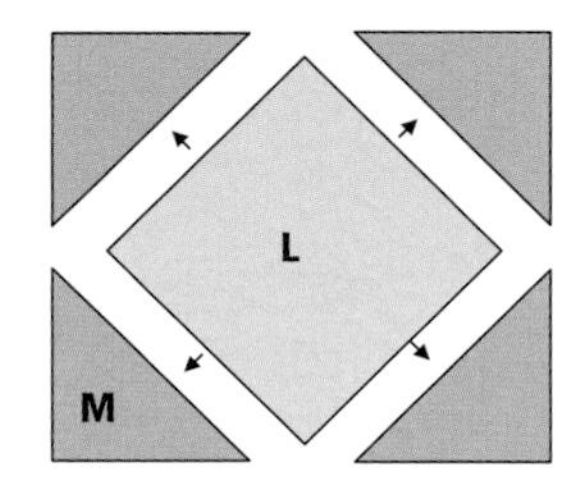

9. To create the third border; sew a border strip (K) to opposite sides of the quilt; press and trim to fit.

10. Measure across finished quilt top including side borders (H and J) only, for top and bottom border length; add ½" to this measurement. Trim two strips (K) to this length. Sew a Diamond in a Square block to each end of the two strips.

11. Sew Diamond in a Square/ K border to top and bottom of quilt, press.

Quilting and Finishing

(See General Instructions page 137–141)

1. Layer and baste together the quilt top, batting, and backing in preparation for quilting.

2. Hand or machine quilt. For the blocks in this quilt, I used invisible nylon thread, stitching in the ditch. For the third border, I free-motion quilted around the floral motifs, loosely outlining the flowers.

3. Finish quilt by cutting and piecing 2¼" strips of straight-grain binding fabric. Sew binding around quilt using folded mitered corners. ❖

Joanna Figueroa

When I bought my first antique quilt at a garage sale, I fell in love with the art of quilting. But when I made my first quilt, I fell in love with the process of quilting. It was as if something "clicked" inside. For me, quilting is a perfect combination of art and practicality; I can be totally creative and totally utilitarian at the same time. Vintage quilts and unusual vintage color combinations inspire most of my designs. I can't seem to go anywhere without seeing patterns or color combinations for potential quilts—in nature, greeting cards, wrapping paper, and dishware.

My favorite quilts utilize a patchwork design that shows off the fabric and color. I am not drawn to complex designs unless they truly showcase a fabric combination in a way that another pattern would not. Whether vintage, soft, bold, contemporary, warm and cuddly, masculine, or romantic, I believe that any feeling can be communicated through a well-chosen palette of color, pattern, and texture.

When I'm not quilting and designing, I am a stay-at-home mom and wife. My two boys, ages one and four, are my joy and take up most of my time. They both believe that all quilts ought to be theirs and feel quite affronted when one is being made that they cannot have! I owe a great deal of my quilting success to my husband, Eric, who is incredibly flexible and acknowledges my need for creative time, my obsession with fabric, and my love for what I do.

Besides quilting, I enjoy searching for vintage textiles, antique toys, painted furniture, and ceramics—anything that seems loved and well used, anything with personality, you might say.

Scarlet Rose Chain

Designed, made, and quilted by Joanna Figueroa
Finished Size: 62" x 62"

I have found that the longer I quilt, the more I fall in love with particular fabrics. When I found this beautiful, vintage-like cream and scarlet floral, I knew it had to be a quilt. I chose the same red as an accent color and started considering patterns. I settled on an Irish Chain variation because I felt that it was the best way to feature such a large, bold floral and still pull out the wonderful red. I used a small floral print for the small pieces surrounding the chain because the floral I had chosen had strong red flower sprays that interfered with the red chain pattern. If you use a uniform all-over floral you will not have this problem. Strip-piecing some of the sections ahead of time made the piecing process much easier and more enjoyable. I used a soft 100% cotton batting because of the vintage, puckered feel it creates when washed.

Materials

Yardage (based on 42" fabric, from selvage to selvage)

Fabric 1: 1¾ yds. red
Fabric 2: 4 yds. medium floral
Fabric 3: 1⅛ yds. large floral
Backing: 4 yds.
Batting: 66" x 66"
Binding: ½ yd.

Cutting Instructions

(See Quilt Layout Diagram)
Cut all fabric crosswise, from selvage to selvage, unless otherwise instructed.

Blocks, Posts, and All Checkerboard Squares

(Fig. 1)

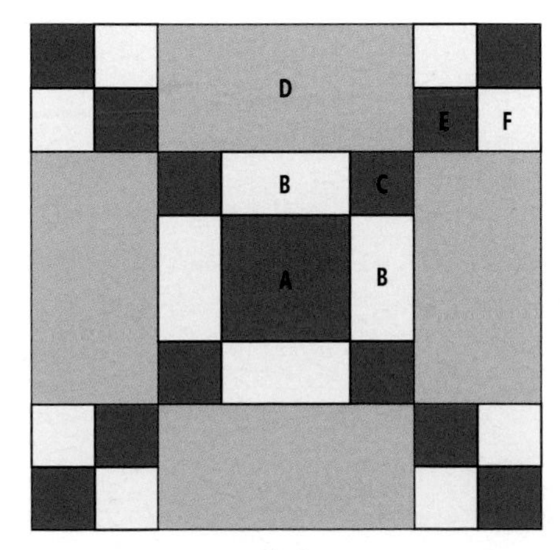

Fig. 1

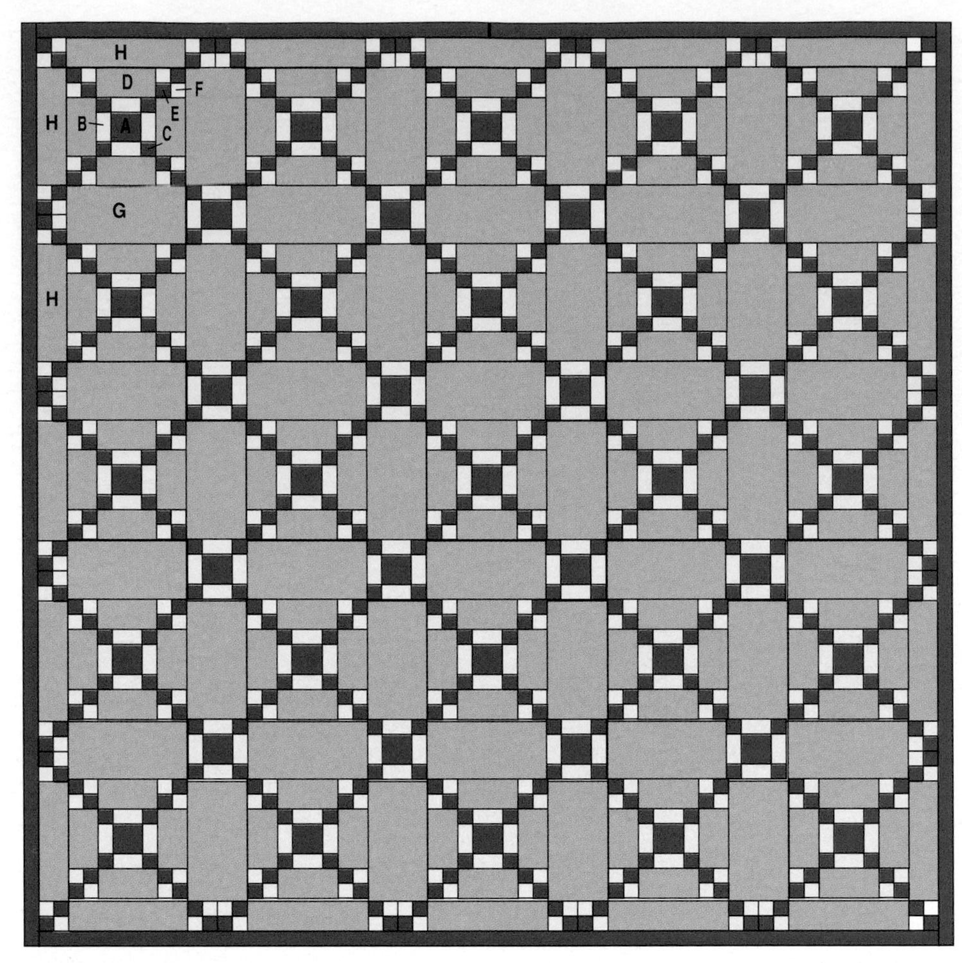

Scarlet Rose Chain Quilt Layout

Fabric 1 - red

Fabric 3 - large floral

Fabric 2 - medium floral

FABRIC 1

PIECE A: Cut three 2½" strips. Then cut strips into (41) 2½" squares.

PIECE C: Cut six 1½" strips.

PIECE E: Cut ten 1½" strips.

FABRIC 2

PIECE F: Cut ten 1½" strips.

PIECE B: Cut six 2½" strips. Then, cut three of these strips into (82) 1½" x 2½" rectangles.

FABRIC 3

PIECE D: Cut seven 4½" strips. Then, cut these strips into (100) 2½" x 4½" rectangles.

Sashing

(See Quilt Layout Diagram)

FABRIC 3

PIECE G: Cut five 8½" strips. Then, cut these strips into (40) 4½" x 8½" rectangles.

Borders

(See Quilt Layout Diagram)

FABRIC 1

PIECE I: Cut eight 1½" strips.

FABRIC 3

PIECE H: Cut five 2½" strips. Then, cut these strips into (20) 2½" x 8½" rectangles.

Binding

Cut seven 2¼" strips.

Construction

Sew ¼" seams with right sides together unless otherwise noted.

Strip-piece units ahead of time for use throughout construction.

Strip-piecing for Block Centers and Posts

1. Sew one 1½" red strip to each side of a 2½" floral strip. Repeat this step three times for a total of three strip sets. Press to the red.

2. Cut the three sets into 1½" units (B/C) (Fig. 2), which will be used in both the blocks and posts. Make 82 units total (50 for the blocks, and 32 for the posts).

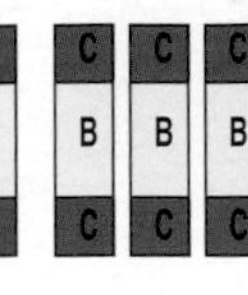

Fig. 2

Scarlet Rose Chain by Joanna Figueroa

Strip-piecing for Checkerboard Units

1. Sew one 1½" red strip to one 1½" medium floral strip. Make ten strip sets. Press to the red. Cut into 1½" E/F units (Fig. 3).

Fig. 3
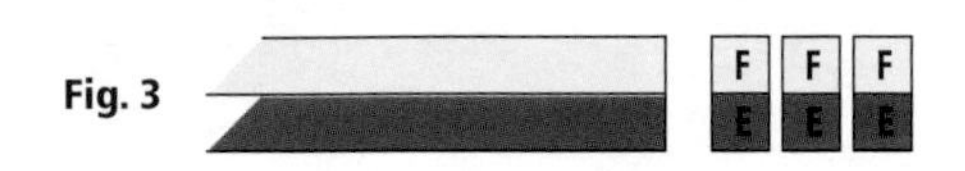

2. Rotate and sew E/F units into a checkerboard pattern (Fig. 4). Make 136 units total (100 for the block corners, and 36 for the borders).

Fig. 4
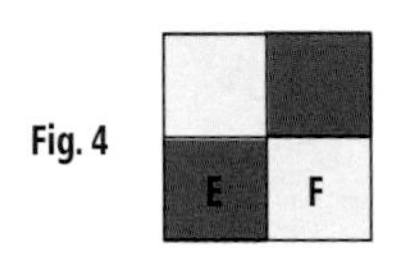

Scarlet Chain

Finished size: 8" x 8"
(See Fig. 1. Make 25 blocks.)

1. Follow the assembly sequence shown in Fig. 5. Referring to Step 1, sew (B) to the top and bottom of (A).

2. Referring to Step 2, sew a B/C unit to each side of the A/B unit. (To save time, make 41 of these units—25 for these blocks, and 16 for the posts. Lay aside the posts until needed).

3. Sew (D) to the top and bottom of each unit (Fig. 5, Step 3). Press toward (D).

4. Sew a strip-pieced checkerboard unit (E/F) to each end of two D pieces (Fig. 5, Step 4). Press toward D. Attach E/F/D units to the sides of the block.

Assembly

1. Alternate and sew together five red chain blocks with four sashing pieces (G) (Fig. 6). Press toward sashings. Make five rows total.

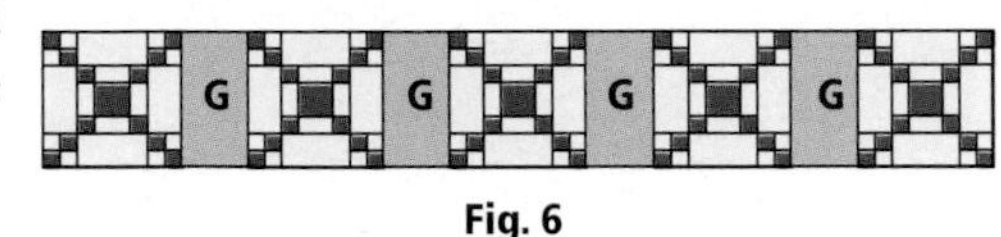

Fig. 6

2. Sew five more sashing pieces (G) with four post squares (strip-pieced earlier) to make sashing rows (Fig. 7). Press toward sashings. Make four sashing rows total.

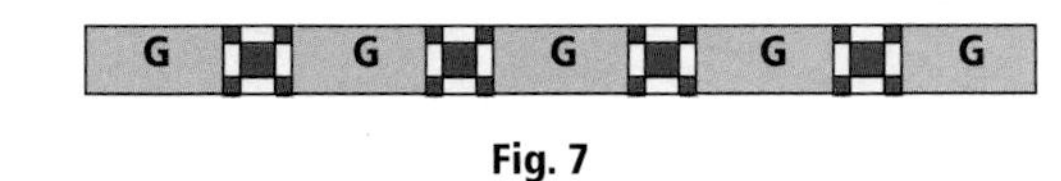

Fig. 7

3. Alternate and sew together the sashing rows and block rows, beginning and ending with a block row.

4. Assemble the top, bottom, and sides of the border, as shown in Fig. 8, with an additional checkerboard on two of the strips. Sew these pieces together, pressing seams toward H.

5. Sew the top and bottom borders to the quilt.

6. Sew the two remaining pieced border strips to the sides of the quilt.

7. To assemble the outer red border, sew together two 1½" red strips for each side, for a total of four sets of two strips each. Measure the width of the top and bottom of the quilt, take the average, and then cut two of the border sets to that length. Pin the sets in place and sew. Press outward. Repeat the process with the two remaining sides, and sew them to the quilt to complete the quilt top.

Quilting and Finishing

(See General Instruction pages 137–141)

1. To create the quilt backing, divide the backing fabric into two 2-yd. pieces and sew them together lengthwise. Your seam will run horizontally.

2. Layer the backing, batting, and quilt top and pin-baste them together. Machine quilt with a small stipple to give the quilt a vintage, puckered appearance. Line-stitch straight through the chain to strengthen the chain pattern.

3. Finish the quilt by piecing 2¼" strips of straight-grain binding fabric. Sew binding around quilt using folded mitered corners. ❖

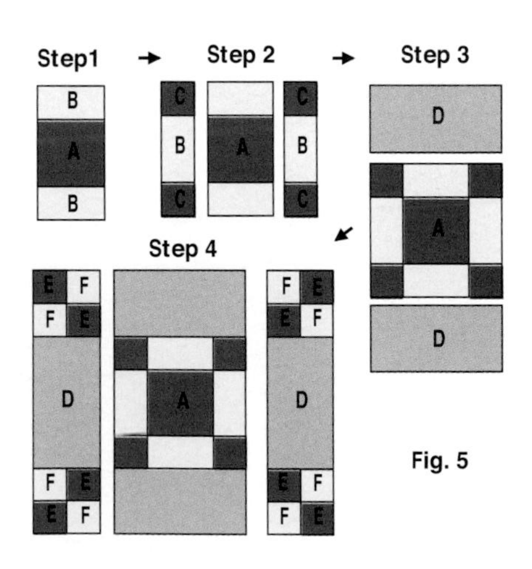

Fig. 5

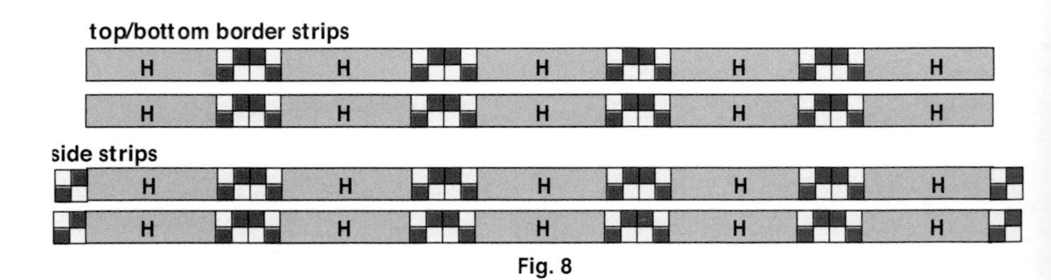

Fig. 8

Marg Gair

I can't remember a time when I didn't love fabric, design, and sewing. One of my earliest sewing recollections as a child is the memory of myself, as a preschooler, dreaming about the opportunity to, one day, sew on my mom's sewing machine. My mom generously shared her sewing machine, her sewing expertise, and her lifelong love of sewing with me.

Although I have always been involved in sewing, I began quilting, quite by accident, about 14 years ago when I was invited to a local quilt guild meeting. Introduced to the world of quiltmaking, it has been my passion ever since. When I attended the meeting, I immediately knew I was surrounded by kindred spirits. The many friends I've met through quilting over the years have been a constant source of encouragement and inspiration. My husband, Steve, my biggest fan, also provides endless support for my quiltmaking.

Traditional and antique quilts have had a strong influence on my quilting style. Although my style of quilting has evolved over the years, I have especially enjoyed making traditional quilts where I usually combine pieced blocks with appliqué. Most recently I have been smitten with the beauty, texture, and sheen of silk fabric so I'm currently off in that direction. Although I think of myself primarily as a quiltmaker, I also enjoy knitting and making miniature, jointed teddy bears.

In addition to teaching quiltmaking, I teach kindergarten part-time. Naturally, my kindergarten class makes a small, simple quilt each year for our class mascots, the three little kittens.

Diamond in a Square

Designed, made, and quilted by Marg Gair
Finished size: 51" x 60"

Although Diamond in a Square begins with a humble, unassuming block, it is transformed into an elegant quilt through the use of silk necktie fabric that provides rich color and interesting texture. Because silk is more difficult to work with than cotton (it lacks stability and frays easily), I used a simple block design for ease of construction. The silk neckties came from a collection that I started several years ago. Once it became known that I was looking for ties, friends, family members, and even strangers began contributing to it. If you don't have a personal collection, you can buy silk tie remnants. You may want to dry clean them first, or you can dry clean your quilt after it is finished. Although laundering is an option, I prefer not to launder silk because the intense colors can bleed and the lovely original sheen of the silk disappears after laundering.

Materials

Yardage (based on 42" fabric, from selvage to selvage)

Fabric 1: 1⅓ yds. total assorted dark silk ties
Fabric 2: 2 yds. total assorted medium silk ties
Fabric 3: ¼ yd. assorted maroon silk ties
Fabric 4: ⅝ yd. assorted blue silk ties
Backing: 3 yds.
Binding: ⅓ yd. assorted ties
Batting: 56" x 64" (thin)
6" square ruler
Lightweight, loosely woven iron-on interfacing (optional)

Cutting

(See Quilt Layout Diagram)

Before cutting silk neckties, take them apart and press them flat. The silk fabric you use may be stable enough to stand on its own without an interfacing. If the silk is fraying or not firmly woven, use a lightweight, loosely woven iron-on interfacing to back the silk fabric before you cut pieces from it.

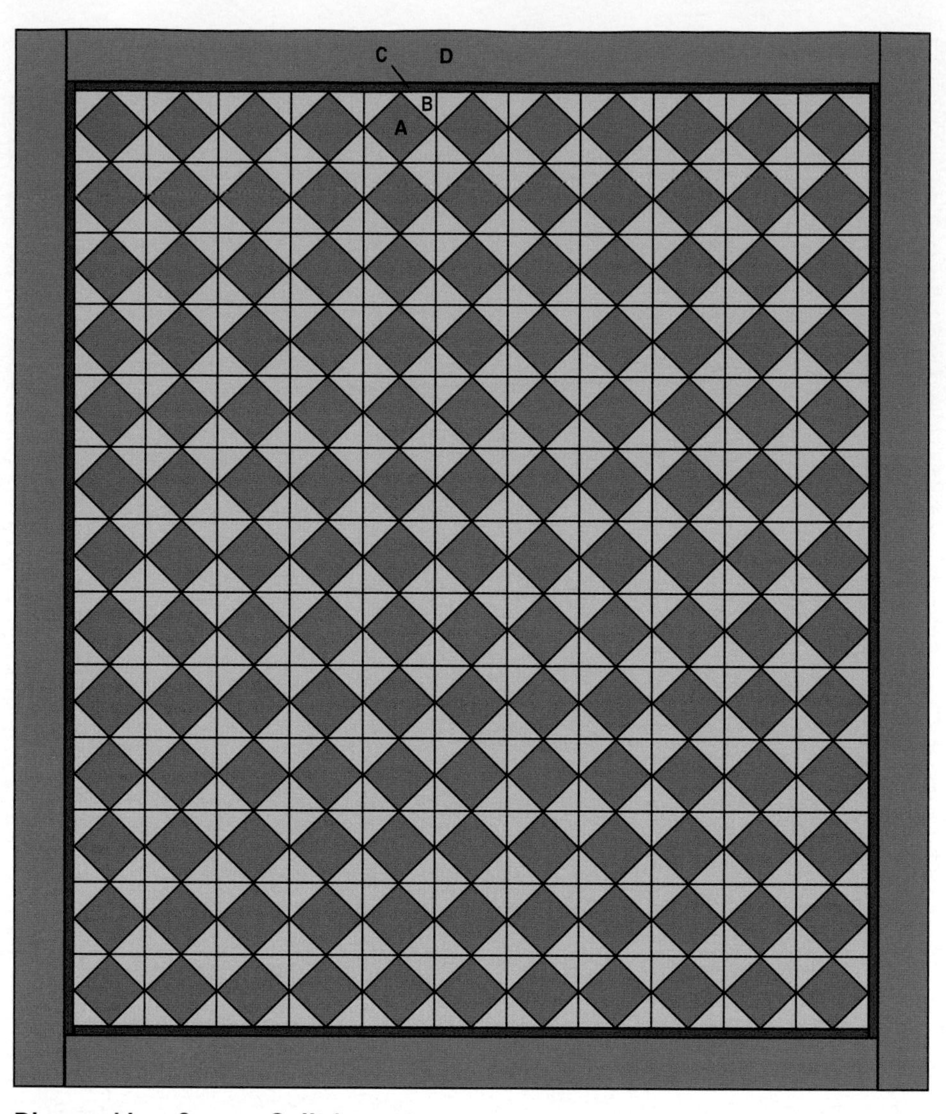

Diamond in a Square Quilt Layout

- Fabric 1 - assorted dark silk ties
- Fabric 2 - assorted medium silk ties
- Fabric 3 - maroon silk ties
- Fabric 4 - assorted blue silk ties

Diamond in a Square

(Fig. 1)

Fig. 1

B

A

FABRIC 1

PIECE A: Cut (143) 3½" squares.

FABRIC 2

PIECE B: Cut (286) 3" squares, and then cut each square on the diagonal to create two triangles. **NOTE:** Each diamond requires four matching triangles, so for each diamond, be sure to cut two 3" squares from the same tie or silk scrap.

Borders

(See Quilt Layout Diagram)

FABRIC 3

PIECE C: Cut five 1" strips for the inner border.

FABRIC 4

PIECE D: Cut six 3" strips for the outer border.

Diamond in a Square by Marg Gair

Construction

Sew ¼" seams with right sides together unless otherwise noted.

Diamond in a Square

Finished size: 4¼" x 4¼"
(See Fig. 1. Make 143 blocks.)

To construct each block:

1. Sew two triangles (B) onto opposite sides of a diamond (A). Then, press the seams toward the triangles; trim points (Fig. 2).

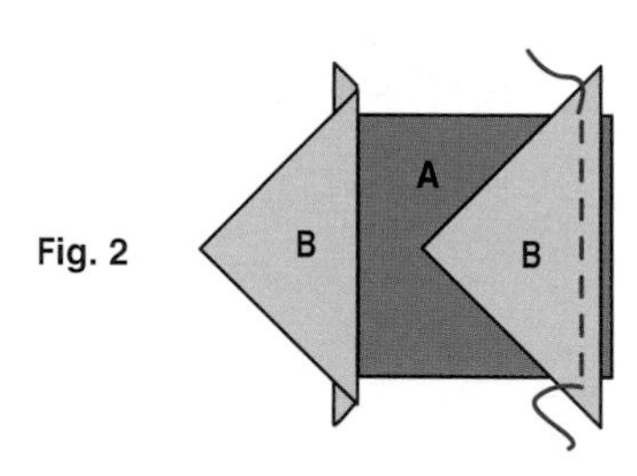

Fig. 2

2. Sew the second two matching triangles (B) onto the remaining sides of the diamond. Then, press the seams toward the triangles; trim points (Fig. 3)

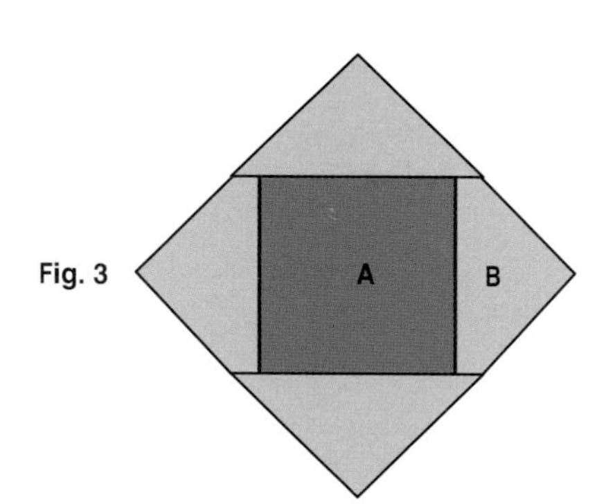

Fig. 3

Assembly

1. Lay out the blocks in a pleasing arrangement, using 11 blocks per row for a total of 13 rows. Sew together the blocks in each row. Press the seams toward the right on odd rows and toward the left on even rows.

2. Sew together the rows, pressing the seams toward the bottom of the quilt. At this point your quilt should measure 47¼" x 55¼".

3. To create the inner border, piece together 1" strips (C) to create two 1" x 49" strips. Sew these strips to the top and bottom of the quilt; trim to fit.

4. Piece together the remaining strips (C) to create two 1" x 59" strips. Sew these strips to the sides of the quilt; trim to fit.

5. To create the outer border, piece together 3" strips (D) to create two 3" x 49" strips. Sew these strips to the top and bottom of the quilt. Trim to fit.

6. Piece together the remaining strips (D) to create two 3" x 63" strips. Sew these strips to the sides of the quilt to complete the quilt top; trim to fit.

Quilting and Finishing

(See General Instructions pages 137–141)

1. Layer and baste together the quilt top, batting, and backing in preparation for quilting.

2. Hand or machine quilt. For this quilt, I machine quilted in the ditch horizontally and vertically. Then I free-motion quilted a circle in the center of each diamond (Fig. 4). I used a purchased stencil to machine quilt a simple serpentine design on the border, but any stencil design would be fine.

Fig. 4

3. Finish the quilt by cutting and piecing 2¼" strips of straight-grain binding fabric. Sew binding around quilt using folded mitered corners.❖

Donna Heppler

I can't think of anything that has brought more meaning and joy to my life—with the exception of my husband and children—than the art of quilting. I remember sitting next to my great Aunt Seal at my grandparents' cabin and watching her stitch through three layers of triangles and wondering, what she was doing. I didn't make my first quilt until the year I was married. My husband gave me my first sewing machine for my nineteenth birthday, and I decided that I would make a quilt. It wasn't the prettiest thing, but my sewing machine worked great, and I've been sewing ever since. My sister, Judy, is also a quilter. I showed her how to sew; she showed me how to use the rotary cutter. I think the rotary cutter is right up there with the discovery of electricity.

I don't personally own a quilt; they've all been given away—to my children, husband, family, and friends. When I make a quilt for somebody, I choose the design, and then I choose the colors. I consider the person receiving the quilt, his or her age, favorite color, or home décor and go from there.

One of the special things for me about quilting is that it brings people, especially women, closer together. My daughters love to pick favorite colors of fabric for their personal stash. I taught my oldest daughter how to sew when she was 13, and I helped her make her first quilt a year later. Since then we've shared the quiltmaking process many times. It is something that we have in common. Through quilting I have met wonderful women who inspire and motivate by sharing their quilt projects. I thank them all.

Pinwheels at Night

Designed, made, and quilted by Donna Heppler
Finished size: 66" x 90"

I have always liked pinwheels. They remind me of being young, with no cares, of just being fascinated by how the wind makes a pinwheel spin. When I first designed this quilt, I used pastels to piece the first block, but I quickly decided to switch to brighter fabrics to achieve a more dramatic effect. Although I have used a wide variety of colors, the white fabric used in every block and the polka dot fabric used in the pinwheel centers, posts, and binding help tie the quilt together and give it a unified look.

Materials

Yardage (based on 42" fabric from selvage to selvage)

Fabric 1:	6 yds. black
Fabric 2:	2 yds. light with polka dots
Fabric 3:	¼ yd. each of 17 assorted brights
Fabric 4:	½ yd. black with polka dots
Batting:	2¼ yds. or pre-packaged twin size
Backing:	6 yds.
Binding:	½ yd.

Cutting

(See Quilt Layout Diagram)
Cut all fabric crosswise, from selvage to selvage, unless otherwise instructed.

Pinwheel Block

(Fig. 1)

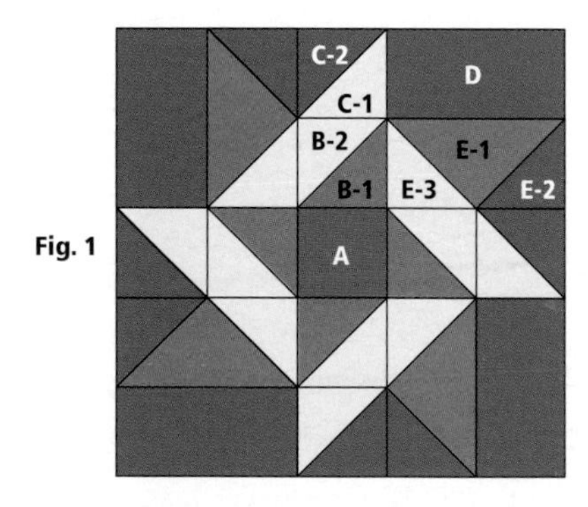

Fig. 1

FABRIC 4

Cut six 2½" strips, then cut as follows:

Piece A: Cut these strips into 2½" squares for a total of 35 squares.

Piece F: Cut the remaining strips into 2½" squares for a total of 48 posts.

FABRIC 3

Piece B-1: Cut two 3" squares from each of the darker brights for a total of 70 squares.

Piece E-1: Cut four 2½" x 4½" rectangles from lighter brights for a total of 140 rectangles.

FABRIC 2

Piece B-2: Cut five 3" strips, and then cut each strip into 3" squares for a total of 70 squares.

Piece C-1: Cut five 3" strips, and then cut each strip into 3" squares for a total of 70 squares.

Piece E-3: Cut nine 2½" strips, and then cut each strip into 2½" squares for a total of 140 squares.

FABRIC 1

Piece C-2: Cut five 3" strips, and then cut each strip into 3" squares for a total of 70 squares.

Piece D: Cut (17) 2½" strips, and then cut each strip into 2½" x 4½" rectangles for a total of 140 rectangles.

Piece E-2: Cut nine 2½" strips, and then cut each strip into 10½" rectangles for a total of 82 rectangles.

Piece G: Cut (21) 2½" strips and then cut each strip into 10½" rectangles for a total of 82 rectangles.

Piece H: Cut nine 2½" strips.

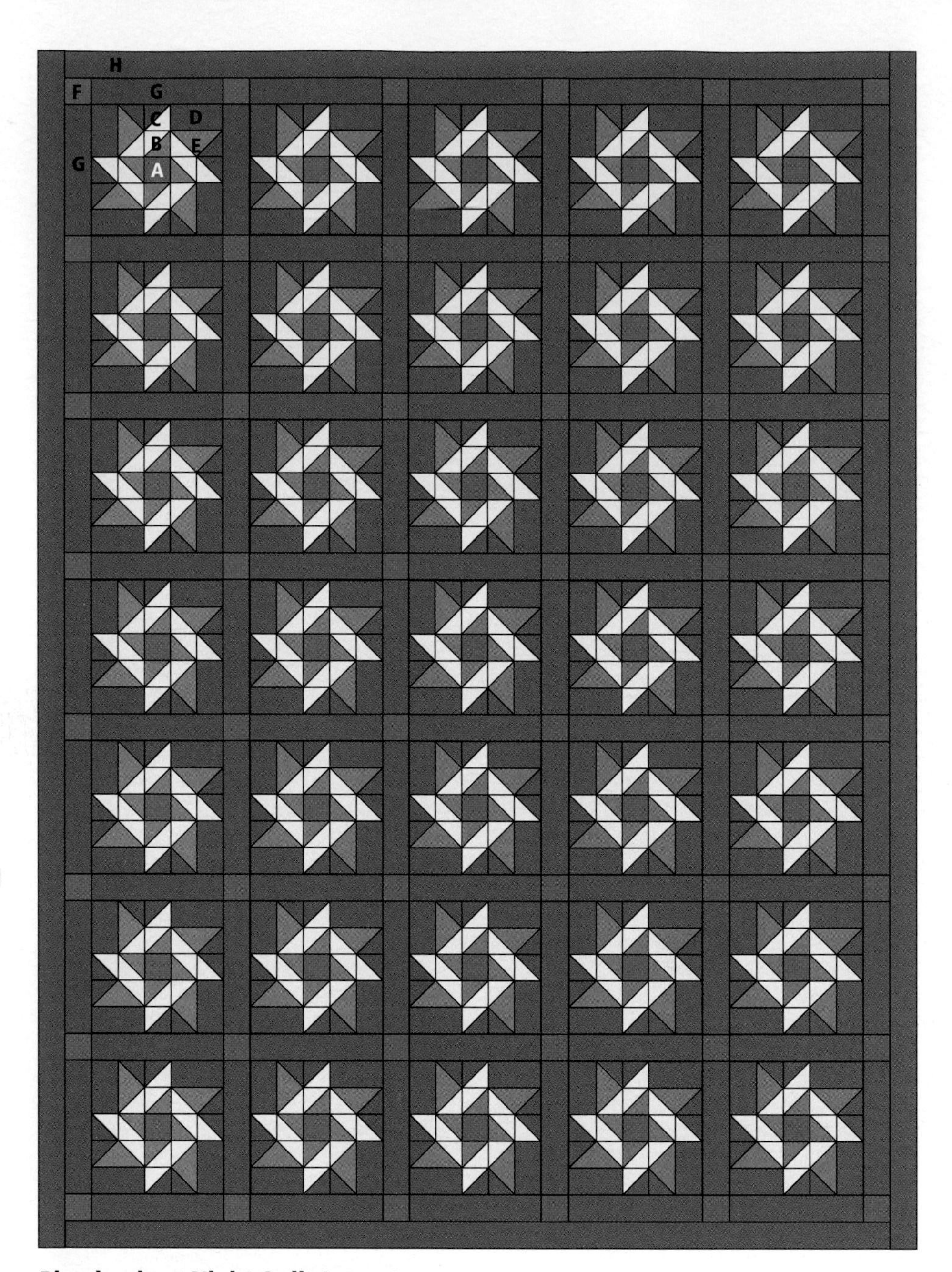

Pinwheels at Night Quilt Layout

Fabric 1 - black

Fabric 2 - light with polka dots

Fabric 3 - assorted brights

Fabric 4 - black with polka dots

To make each pinwheel block:

1. Place Piece B-1 on top of Piece B-2, right sides together; draw a line diagonally across the square. Stitch along both sides of the line (Fig. 2), and then cut along the line (Fig. 3). Open the two resulting squares and press (Fig. 4). The finished squares should be 2½"; if not, square them up with a ruler. Using the same fabric, repeat this step to create a total of four B units (half-square triangles) for each block.

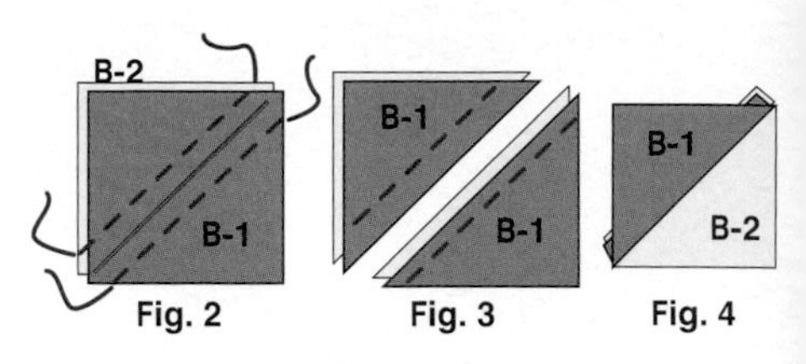

Fig. 2 Fig. 3 Fig. 4

2. Use the same method as in Step 1 for Pieces C-1 and C-2 to create a total of four C units (half-square triangles) for each block.

3. Place Piece E-2 over the left side of Piece E-1, right sides together. Stitch across Piece E-2 on the diagonal (Fig. 5). Cut away the resulting outside triangle (Fig. 6) until it is ¼" from the seam; open the E-2/E-1 unit, and press.

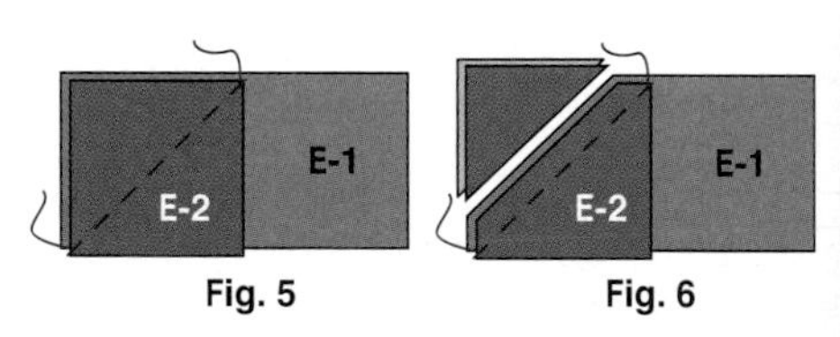

Fig. 5 Fig. 6

4. Place Piece E-3 over the right side of the E-2/E-1 unit (Fig. 7) and use the same method as in Step 3 to complete a double half-square triangle (Fig. 8). Repeat Steps 3 and 4 to create a total of four E units (double half-square triangles) for each block.

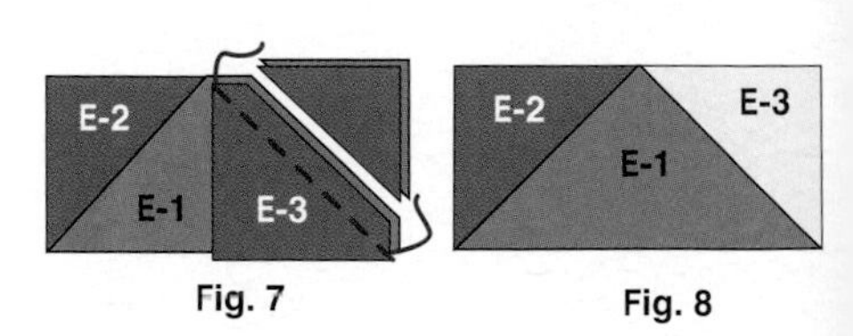

Fig. 7 Fig. 8

5. Sew together a finished E unit and Piece D, stitching along the long edge of the large triangle (E-1). Open the sewn unit and press the seam toward Piece D. Repeat this step to create a total of four D/E units for each block.

Pinwheels at Night by Donna Heppler

6. Sew together the B and C units, being sure to stitch along the B-2/C-1 edge. Open and press. Repeat this step to create a total of four B/C units for each block.

To piece the units:

7. Lay out each block as shown in Fig. 9. Join units in rows, pressing seams to outside in direction of arrows.

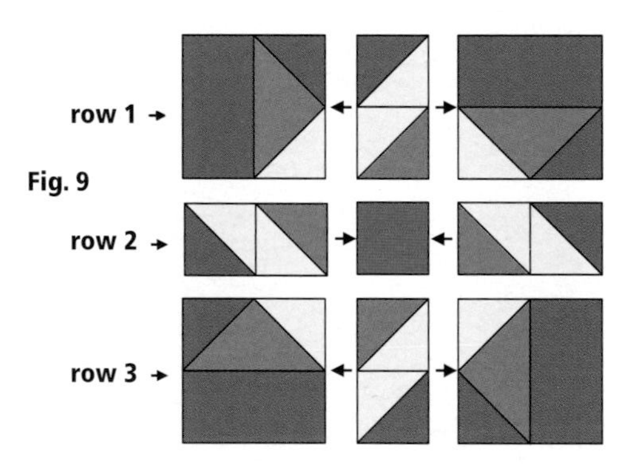

Fig. 9

8. Sew rows together. Press seams toward outside rows.

Assembly

(See Quilt Layout Diagram)

1. Lay out pinwheel blocks in a pleasing arrangement. Alternate and sew together six sashing and five pinwheel blocks to make a row of pinwheels, starting and ending with sashing. Repeat to create seven pinwheel rows (Fig. 10) Press each row's seams in an alternating direction.

2. Alternate and sew together six posts (F) and five strips of sashing (G), starting and ending with a post (Fig. 11). Repeat to create eight sashing rows.

3. Lay out the sashing rows and pinwheel rows, starting and ending with a sashing row. Then, sew the rows to the pinwheel rows, being sure to align sashing with posts.

To create the border:

Note: Be sure to check the actual finished width and length of your quilt before cutting these strips, and then adjust Step 4 and Step 5 strip's measurements, if necessary.

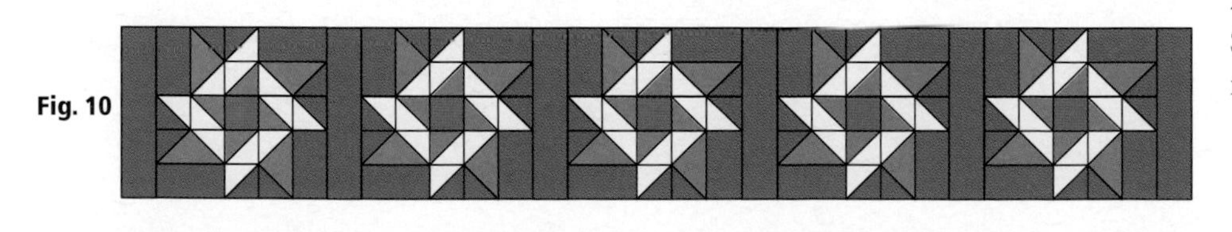
Fig. 10

Fig. 11

4. Piece together the border strips (H) to create two 2½" x 66" strips. Attach these strips to the quilt top and bottom.

5. Piece together the remaining border strips (H) to create two 2½" x 90" strips and sew to the sides of the quilt.

Quilting and Finishing

(See General Instructions pages 137–141)

1. Layer and baste together the quilt top, batting, and backing in preparation for quilting.

2. Hand or machine quilt. I machine quilted this quilt using a meandering stitch on the outside of the pinwheels and a stippling stitch inside the pinwheels. I thought these stitches went well with the theme of the fabric and the pattern of the quilt.

3. Finish the quilt by cutting and piecing 2¼" strips of straight-grain binding fabric. Sew binding around quilt using folded mitered corners. ❖

Sandy Klop

A LITTLE BLACK, CLAMPED-TO-THE-TABLE, HAND-CRANKED SINGER WAS MY FIRST sewing machine. I got it for Christmas when I was eight. I soon graduated to my grandmother's treadle machine, which my mother had converted to electric. On those two machines, I made lots of doll clothes and clothes for myself. Several machines have come and gone, but those two are still in my collection.

I began quilting in 1979. Soon I was making pattern samples for a local quilt store. From there, I moved to doing machine quilting for the store on my Bernina. I'm now on my second commercial quilting machine, and I quilt full-time in my studio at home. Since 1990, I have worked in local quilt stores, taught classes, and have had a drop-in sewing class for people who want to work on their quilt projects.

I am passionate about quilting and the quilters I meet. I love the stories of quilt tops found in attics or garage sales, quilts made by a generation past, and new grandmothers making their first quilts for an expected baby. Comfort quilts made for patients or victims make me think this is a great business to be in.

I have machine-quilted thousands of quilts and made hundreds, in styles from traditional to story to folk art. I have had quilts displayed at the Houston Quilt Show and the Pacific International Quilt Festival (PIQF). In 2001 and 2002, I published a series of three quilt books called *Folk Art Favorites* with Jan Patek.

Cheery Cherry

Designed, made, and quilted by Sandy Klop
Finished size: 68" x 68"

The pattern for this quick and easy quilt is a simple log cabin (courthouse step construction) using the same fabric for each round. When choosing your fabrics, decide on a theme such as green/red/white, brights, novelty fabrics, reproduction prints, florals, plaids, checks, or stripes. Be sure to include light, dark, and medium tones and choose prints, plaids, and stripes in a variety of scales. For this quilt's theme, I chose a cherry print that had red bric-a-brac, and then accentuated the theme with greens, reds, whites, and blacks. If you are planning to make a quilt with fewer than 12 blocks, either make two quilts or sew with a friend so that you will have a greater variety of fabrics.

Materials

(Yardage based on 42" fabric, from selvage to selvage)

Begin by deciding the size of your quilt.

Quilt as shown with a 4½" border
  68" square: 16 block (15" x 15")
Table top with a 6" border
  42" square: 4 blocks (2 x 2)
Crib without a border
  45" x 60": 12 blocks (3 x 4)
Twin with 8" border
  76" x 91": 20 blocks (4 x 5)
Queen with 8" border
  91" square: 25 blocks (5 x 5)
King without border
  120" square: 64 blocks (8 x 8)

Fabric 1: ⅛ yd. cherry fabric for every 12 blocks; 2 yds. for the border (1 yd., if pieced)
Fabric 2*: ¼ yd. per block
Backing: 4 yds.**
Binding: ½ yd.**
Batting: 72" square**

** Buy as many different valued and patterned fabrics as you have blocks, plus one additional fabric for the center and border. For example, for a quilt with 16 blocks, buy 17 different fabrics.*

*** For 68" x 68" quilt shown.*

Cutting

Instructions given are for the 68" x 68" quilt shown. Cut all strips crosswise, from selvage to selvage, unless otherwise noted.

Log Cabin Block

(Fig. 1)

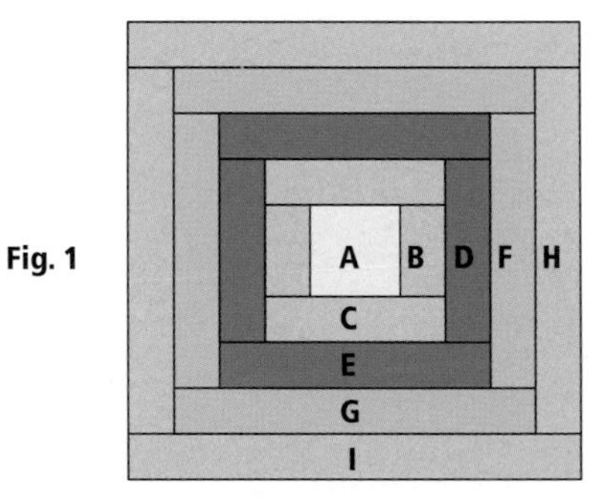

FABRIC 1

Piece A: Cut one 3½" square for each block. Set aside in Stack A.

Piece J: Cut two 4¾" x 62" strips* lengthwise.

Piece K: Cut two 4¾" x 70" strips* lengthwise.

**For other quilt sizes using a 4¼" border, measure the width of the quilt through its center. Then, cut the two strips (J) to the width (x) of the quilt. Cut two strips (K) to the quilt length plus 9".*

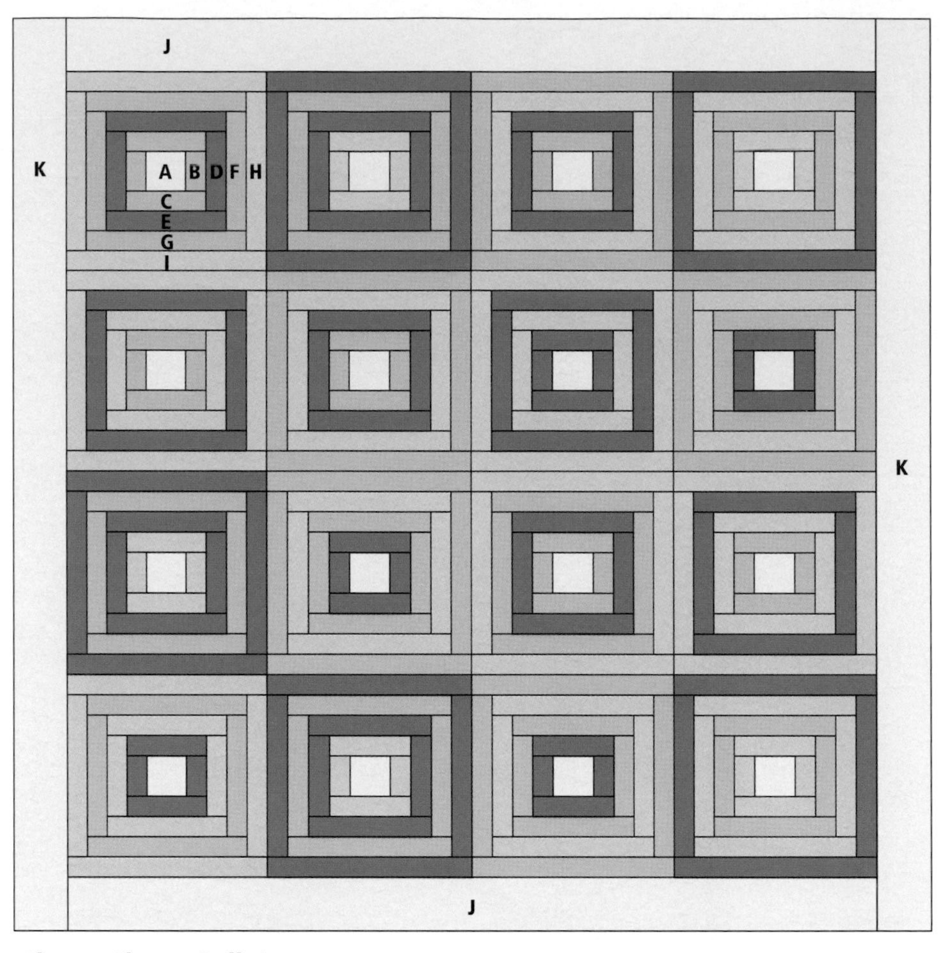

Cheery Cherry Quilt Layout

Fabric 1 – cherry print

Fabric 2 – assorted values and prints*

Fabric 2 – assorted values and prints*

Fabric 2 – assorted values and prints*

*See Materials List

FABRIC 2

From each of the log fabrics, cut four 2" strips. With a sharp blade you may be able to cut as many as eight layers (four fabrics) at one time.

Fold the four strips in half and lay them horizontally on your cutting board (Fig. 2). Trim off all selvages. Then, cut each set of four strips and set them aside in stacks as indicated.

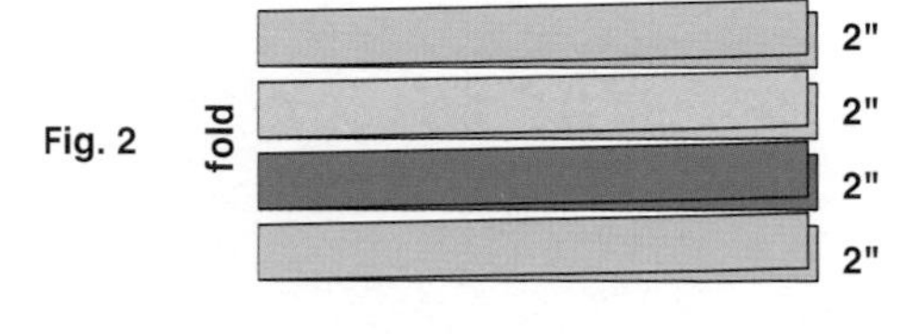

Fig. 2

From the first strip:

PIECE B: Cut two 2" x 3½" pieces (logs). Set aside in Stack B.

PIECE I: Cut two 2" x 15½" logs. Set aside in Stack I.

From the second strip:

PIECE C: Cut two 2" x 6½" logs. Set aside in Stack C.

PIECE G: Cut two 2" x 12½" logs. Set aside in Stack G.

From the third strip:

PIECE D: Cut two 2" x 6½" logs. Set aside in Stack D.

PIECE H: Cut two 2" x 12½" logs. Set aside in Stack H.

From the fourth strip:

PIECE E: Cut one 2" x 9½" log. Set aside in Stack E.

PIECE F: Cut one 2" x 9½" log. Set aside in Stack F.

When you have cut all of your fabrics you should have nine stacks (A through I):

One stack of center squares (A)
One stack of 2" x 3½" logs (B)
Two stacks of 2" x 6½" logs (C and D)
Two stacks of 2" x 9½" logs (E and F)
Two stacks of 2" x 12½" logs (G and H)
One stack of 2" x 15½" logs (I)

Cheery Cherry by Sandy Klop

Construction

Sew ¼" seams with right sides together unless otherwise noted.

Log Cabin Blocks

Finished size: 15" x 15"

(See Fig. 1.)

1. Use the Chain piecing method to assemble the blocks. Begin with the stack of center squares (A) and the stack of 2" x 3½" logs (B). Sew the first log (B) onto a center square; set the second log (B) aside. Without cutting the thread, sew together another center square (A) and another log (B), again setting the second log (B) aside. Continue this process until you have used all the center squares (Fig. 3). Keep the logs in the order you set them aside.

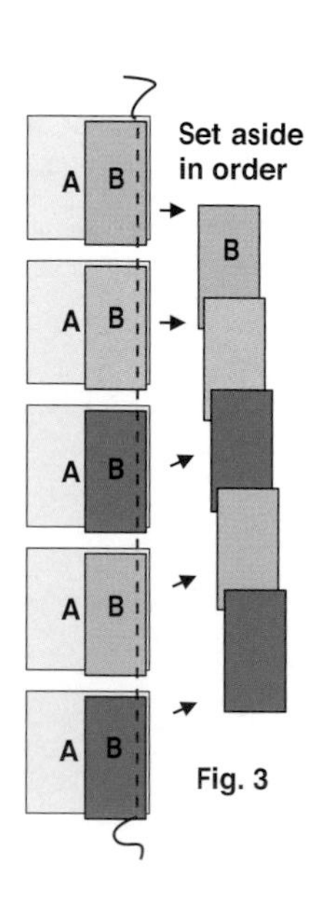

Fig. 3

2. Turn around the strip of A/B units and sew the matching log (B) to the opposite side of each square. When you have finished, clip the threads between the squares and press away from the center.

3. Repeat this process for the first stack of 2" x 6½" logs (C), sewing one log (C) to the AB/unit and setting one log aside. Be sure that the log fabric (C) sewn to each A/B unit is the same as the fabric used in the first log (B). When you reach the end, turn around the strip and sew on the second log (C) to the opposite side of the A/B unit. When you reach the end, clip between the units and press to complete Round 1 of your quilt.

4. To create Round 2, use a coordinating fabric from the second stack of 2" x 6½" logs (D). Use the process given in Steps 1 and 2, being sure to sew the new log (D) to the side with the shorter log (B), not the same size log (C).

5. To complete Round 2, repeat the process given in Step 3, using the first stack of 2" x 9½" logs (E).

6. To create Round 3, repeat the process given in Steps 4–5, using the second stack of 2" x 9½" logs (F) and the first stack of 2" x 12½" logs (G).

7. To create Round 4, repeat process given in Steps 4–5, using the second stack of 2" x 12½" logs (H) and the stack of 2" x 15½" logs (I).

Assembly

1. Lay out the finished blocks in a pleasing arrangement. Sew together the blocks to create the desired number of rows. Press the first block to the left and the next block to the right; continue to alternate the pressing direction for each block.

2. Sew together the rows and press.

3. To create the border, sew strip (J) to the top and bottom of the quilt; press and trim to fit.

4. Sew the next two strips (K) to sides of the quilt; press and trim to fit.

Quilting and Finishing

(See General Instructions pages 137–141)

1. Layer and baste together the quilt top, batting, and backing in preparation for quilting.

2. Hand or machine quilt. For this quilt, I stitched in the ditch around the logs and stippled the borders.

3. Finish the quilt by cutting and piecing 2¼" strips of straight-grain binding fabric. Sew binding around quilt using folded mitered corners.❖

Lori LeVar

I grew up in central Illinois where I met and married my high school sweetheart. We have three teenage children and live in the East Bay, near San Francisco. My first sewing project was a dress my mother taught me to make when I was eight years old. Over the years I have enjoyed many crafts, including counted cross-stitch, needlepoint, calligraphy, decorator window treatments, and of course quilting. I made my first quilt 20 years ago—a baby quilt for my first child.

When my husband and our family moved to the Middle East (Kuwait and U.A.E.) for four years, I was involved with the American Women's League, where I started a quilt group. From there we moved to Franklin, Tennessee, and then to my childhood hometown in Illinois. Shortly after that my husband's job transferred us again, this time to Tokyo, Japan where we lived for five years. In Tokyo, a friend and I combined our talents to make more than a dozen banners for Tokyo International Baptist Church where our families attended.

It was during the years in Japan that my love for quilting was revived. I loved learning about the Japanese indigo fabrics, the dyeing process, and other Japanese textiles such as the kimono and obi fabrics. I was in two quilt groups there, and in one of these groups I learned to hand appliqué. The result was a queen-sized Baltimore Album quilt, with each block hand-appliquéd.

I work at ThimbleCreek where I also teach quilt classes and enjoy preparing store models and Block-of-the-Month kits. I am a member of Diablo Valley Quilt Guild and belong to a monthly quilting group, "Sew What." Spring Medallion is my first original quilt design.

Spring Medallion

Designed and made by Lori Le Var; quilted by Ginger Hayes
Finished size: 71" x 71"

I designed Spring Medallion specifically for this book. I wanted to make a square quilt, like a round robin, but one in which I created each new border. My love of blue-and-white fabric stems from my years of collecting blue-and-white dishes and fabric while living in Japan. I have always liked the traditional Sawtooth Star pattern and chose to make a pinwheel in the center of the quilt to catch attention. I mitered the corners of the quilt to reinforce the quilt's symmetrical look and to give the impression of the borders radiating outward. The bright pink dot fabric was incorporated to give the quilt a carefree feel.

Materials

Yardage (based on 42" fabric, from selvage to selvage)

Fabric 1: 1¼ yds. red (includes binding)
Fabric 2: ⅜ yd. medium light blue
Fabric 3: ⅜ yd. medium blue
Fabric 4: ⅞ yd. light blue
Fabric 5: ⅜ yd. medium dark blue
Fabric 6: ½ yd. dark blue
Fabric 7: 2¼ yds. floral print
Fabric 8: 1 yd. medium gold
Fabric 9: ⅝ yd. light gold
Fabric 10: ⅜ yd. dark gold
Fabric 11: 1⅝ yds. blue stripe
Fabric 12: ¾ yd. green
Backing: 4 yds.
¼" bias bar

Cutting

(See Quilt Layout Diagram)
Cut all strips selvage to selvage, unless otherwise instructed.
Note: *To more easily keep track of pieces, you may prefer to cut the star and border pieces as you construct each star or border.*

Medallion Center Star

(Fig. 1)

Fig. 1

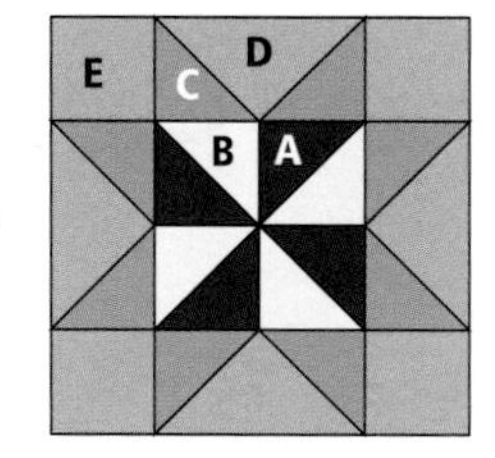

FABRIC 1
Piece A: Cut two 2⅞" squares.

FABRIC 9
Piece B: Cut two 2⅞" squares.

FABRIC 2
Piece C: Cut eight 2½" squares.

FABRIC 11
Piece D: Cut four 2½" x 4½" rectangles.
Piece E: Cut four 2½" squares.

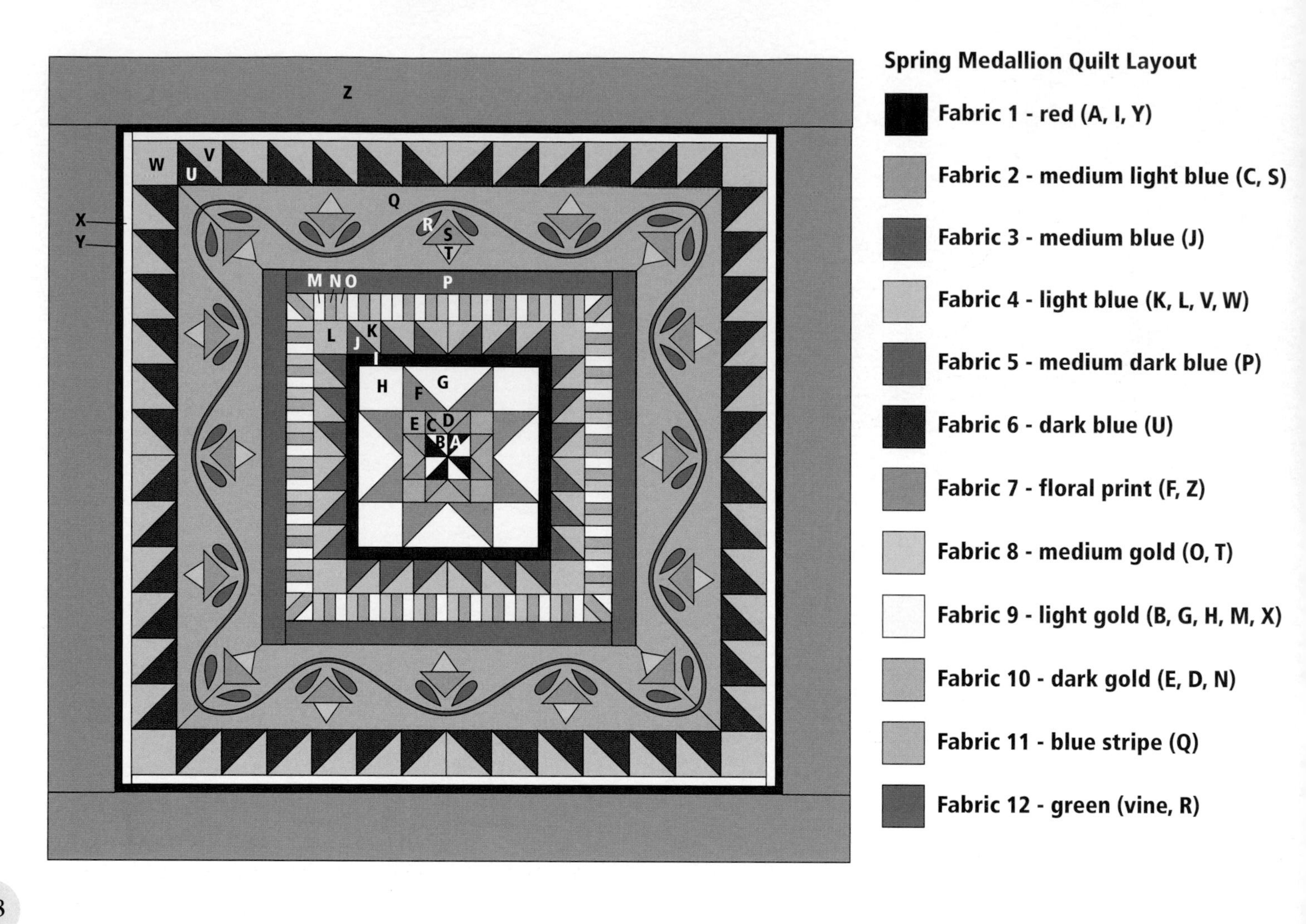

Medallion Second Star

(Fig. 2)

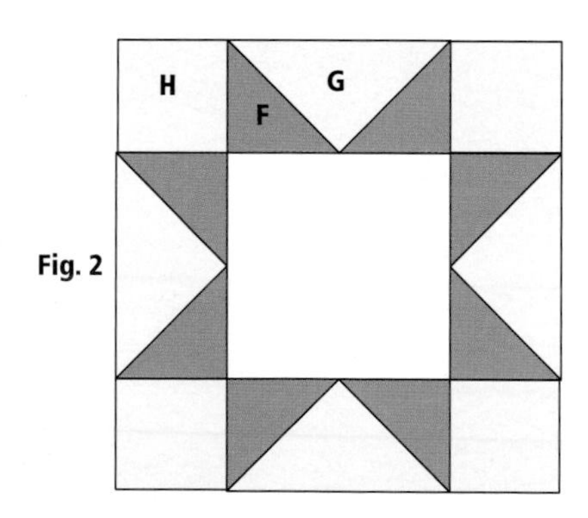

FABRIC 7

Piece F: Cut eight 4½" squares.

FABRIC 9

Piece G: Cut four 4½" x 8½" rectangles.
Piece H: Cut four 4½" squares.

Star Frame Border I

FABRIC I

Piece I: Cut two 1½" x 18" strips and two 1½" x 20" strips.

Small Sawtooth Border

(Fig. 3)

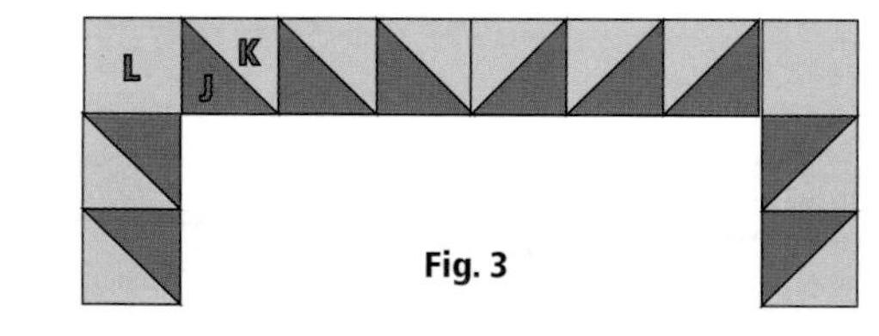

FABRIC 3

Piece J: Cut (12) 3⅞" squares.

FABRIC 4

Piece K: Cut (12) 3⅞" squares.
Piece L: Cut four 3½" squares.

Tri-color Border

(Fig. 4)

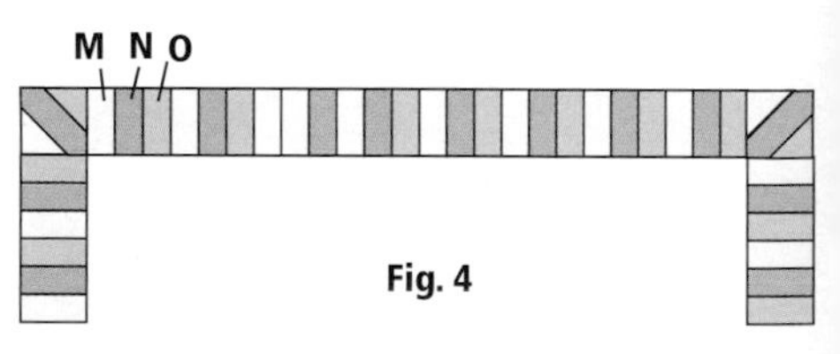

FABRIC 9

Piece M: Cut three 1½" strips. Cut one 2" x 15" strip.

FABRIC 10

Piece N: Cut three 1½" strips. Cut one 1½" x 15" strip.

FABRIC 8

Piece O: Cut three 1½" strips. Cut one 2" x 15" strip.

Spring Medallion by Lori Le Var

Frame Border X
(See Quilt Layout Diagram)

FABRIC 9
PIECE X: Cut six 1¼" strips.

Frame Border Y
(See Quilt Layout Diagram)

FABRIC 1
PIECE Y: Cut six 1" strips.

Construction and Assembly
Sew ¼" seams with right sides together unless otherwise noted.

Medallion Center Star
(See Fig. 1)

1. To create the pinwheel, place one dark square (A) on top of one light square (B). Draw a diagonal line on the top square. Stitch a line ¼" away from both sides of the diagonal line. Cut along the diagonal line (Fig. 5). Open the resulting square, press toward Piece A, and trim points. Repeat for remaining A and B squares.

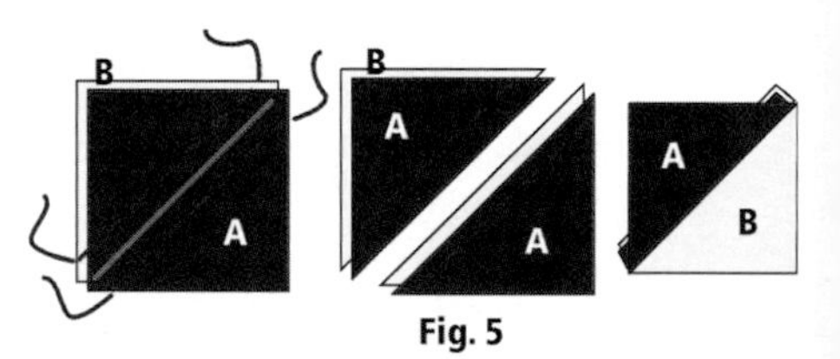

Fig. 5

2. Sew the pinwheel together, being sure to join dark sides to light sides as shown (Fig. 6). Press in the direction of arrows. The resulting pinwheel square should measure 4½".

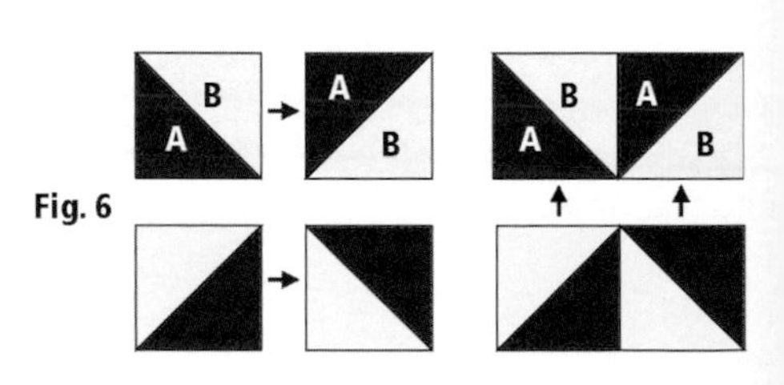

Fig. 6

Frame Border P
(See Quilt Layout Diagram)

FABRIC 5
PIECE P: Cut two 2½" x 32" strips and two 2½" x 36" strips.

Appliqué Border
(See Quilt Layout Diagram)

FABRIC 11
PIECE Q: Cut four 8½" x 54" strips, from length of fabric.

FABRIC 12
For the green vine: Cut ½"-wide strips, and piece to make a 220" long strip. Use a ¼" bias bar and follow package directions for making vine.
PIECE R: Make a template using leaf template (R) on page 62. Use Template R to cut 32 leaves.

FABRIC 2
PIECE S: Cut eight 3" squares (or eight 3⅞" squares if you are using a hand appliqué method), and then cut the squares on the diagonal to create 16 triangles for the flower bases.

FABRIC 8
PIECE T: Make a 4¼" circle template (see General Instructions page 132). Use template to cut 16 circles for the flower buds (T).

Large Sawtooth Border
(See Quilt Layout Diagram)

FABRIC 4
PIECE V: Cut (24) 4⅞" squares.
PIECE W: Cut four 4½" squares.

FABRIC 6
PIECE U: Cut (24) 4⅞" squares.

3. Draw a diagonal pencil line on the wrong side of all eight star point squares (C). Place one square (C) on top of one background rectangle (D) on the left corner (Fig. 7). Sew on the pencil line. Trim the seam allowance to ¼" and trim points. Repeat this process for all four rectangles (D).

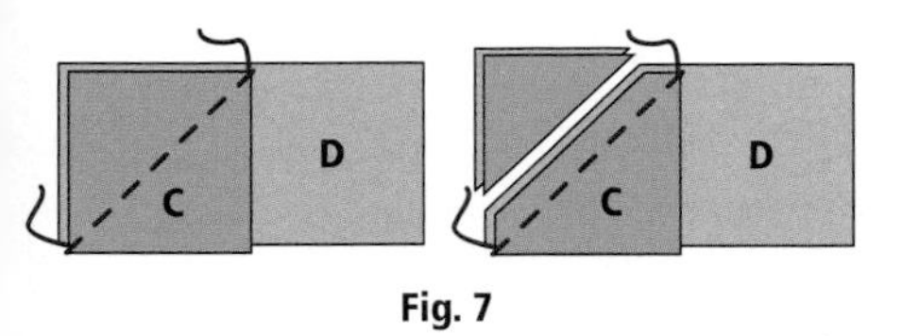

Fig. 7

4. Place another square (C) on the right corner of a C/D unit (Fig. 8) and proceed as for Step 3. Repeat this process for all four rectangles.

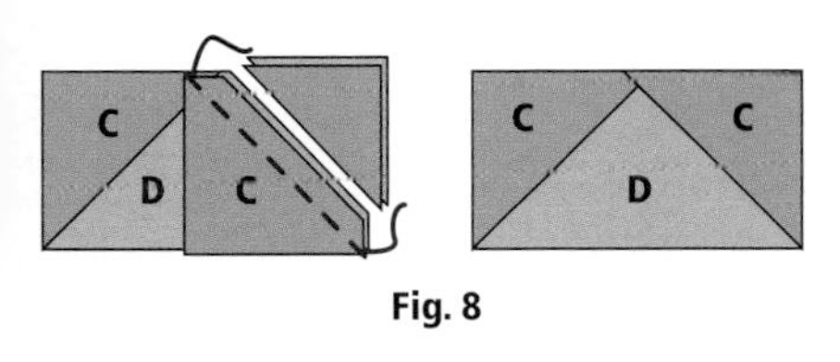

Fig. 8

5. Sew together the star in rows (Fig. 9), using Piece E in the corners and press in the direction of arrows.

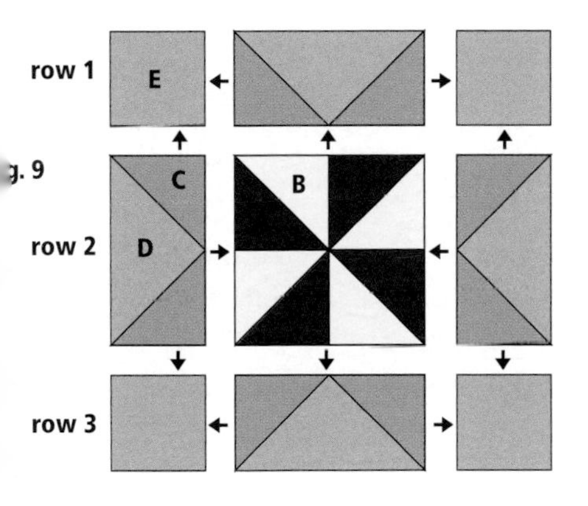

Fig. 9

Medallion Second Star

(See Fig. 2)

To create the large star block, use Steps 3, 4, and 5 above, except replace Pieces C, D, and E with Pieces F, G, and H, respectively, and use the small star block as the center section of the large star block.

Star Frame Border I

(See Quilt Layout Diagram)

To create the star frame border, sew the shorter Border strips (I) to the top and bottom of the star block. Press seam toward the border; trim to fit. Sew the remaining longer strips to the sides of the block, pressing seam toward the border; trim to fit.

Small Sawtooth Border

(See Fig. 3)

1. To create the small sawtooth border, draw a diagonal line on each of the 12 light squares (K), then place each square on top of a dark square (J). Stitch ¼" away from both sides of the diagonal line as in Fig. 5. Cut on the line, press the seam toward the dark square (J), and trim points. Repeat to create a total of (24) 3½" half-square triangles.

2. Sew together four sets of three half-square triangles with the dark triangle on the bottom left side (Set A) and four sets of three half-square triangles with the dark triangle on the bottom right side (Set B).

3. Sew Set A to Set B, with light sides together (Fig. 10). Make four of these strips. Sew two of the strips on opposite sides of the star block. Sew the 3½" squares (L) to each end of the two remaining strips, and then sew these strips to the remaining two sides of the block.

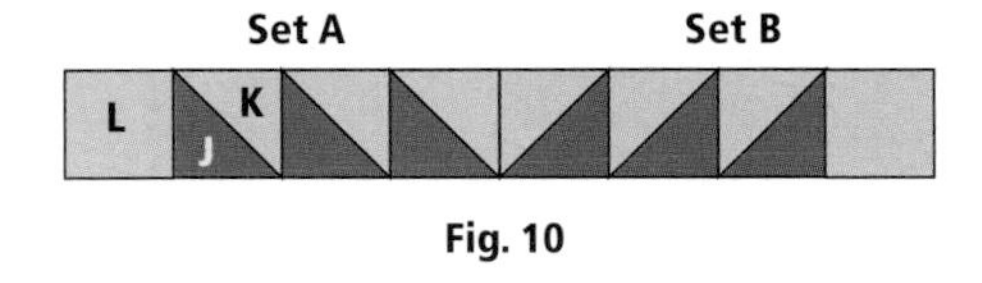

Fig. 10

Tri-color Border

(See Fig. 4)

1. To create the tri-color border, sew together one of each strip (M, N, and O) lengthwise. Create a total of three sets of full-length M/N/O strips and one set of 15" M/N/O strips. Cut apart three strips of the full-length M/N/O units every 3" (Fig. 11) for a total of 32 sets.

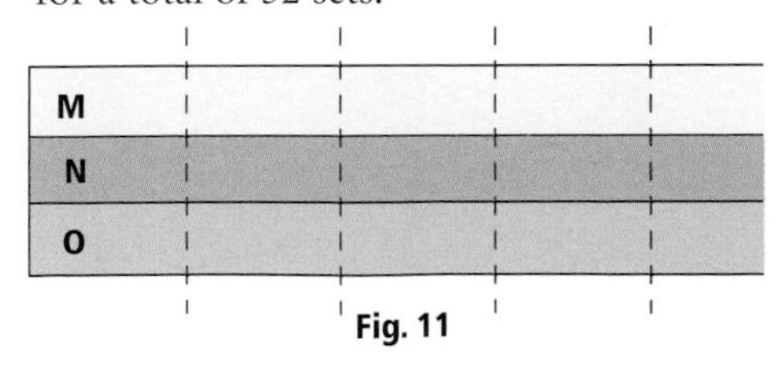

Fig. 11

2. With the remaining 15" M/N/O strip unit, cut four 3½" squares on the bias, centering the points of the square on the middle strip (Fig. 12).

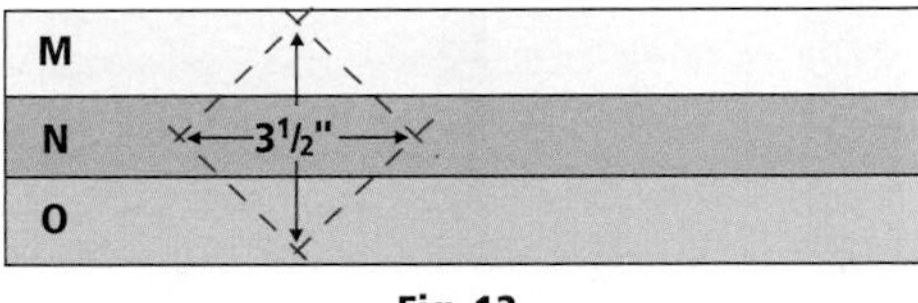

Fig. 12

3. Sew together eight sets of M/N/O units to create each side of the border.

4. Sew two of the finished strips to opposite sides of the star block.

5. Sew the 3½" bias squares to each end of the two remaining border sides. Sew these strips to the remaining sides of the quilt.

Frame Border P

To create the frame border, sew the shorter Border strips (P) to the top and bottom of the quilt; trim to fit. Then sew the two remaining strips (P) to the sides of the quilt; trim to fit.

Appliqué Border

(See Quilt Layout Diagram)

1. To create the background for the appliqué border, find the halfway point on all four sides of the quilt and mark with a pin. Find the halfway point on the Border strips (Q) and mark with a pin. Pin the border strips (Q) to the quilt top, matching center points first and then pinning the border to the sides of the quilt top. Do not pin the overhanging ends of the border. These will be mitered. Sew each border strip to the quilt top, beginning and ending the stitching ¼" from the raw edges of the quilt top.

2. Place the first corner to be mitered on the ironing board. Leave one border laying flat and fold the other one under at a 45-degree angle to the first strip. Press the fold with an iron (Fig. 13A).

3. Fold the quilt, right sides together, on the diagonal, and then line up the edges of the border. If needed, use a ruler to draw a line on the pressed fold to make it more visible. Stitch on the fold, sewing from the corner to the outside edge. Press the seam open and trim away excess border strips leaving a ½" seam allowance (Fig. 13B). Repeat Steps 2 and 3 to miter the remaining corners.

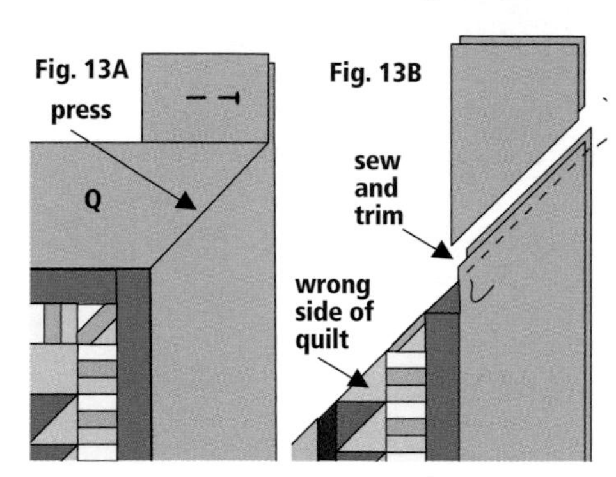

4. To create the appliqué design, fold the flower bud circles (T) in half, and then in thirds (Fig. 14), if necessary press. Use quilt layout for placement of the vine and flower bases (S), buds (T), and leaves (R). Hand or machine appliqué into place (see General Instructions pages 134–135).

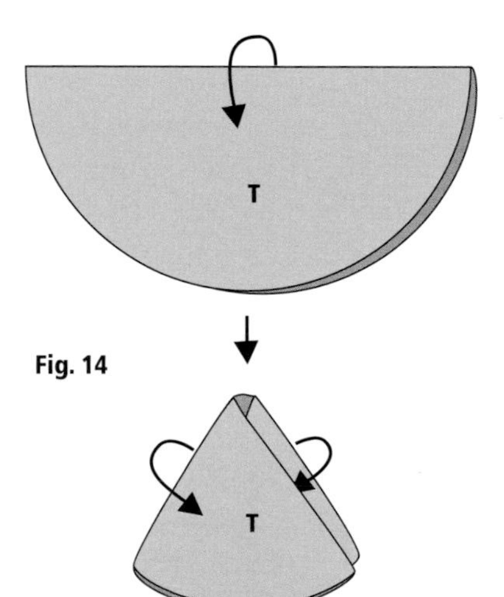

Fig. 14

Large Sawtooth Border

(See Quilt Layout Diagram)

To create the large sawtooth border, use the instructions for Small Sawtooth Border (Steps 1-3), with the following changes:

1. Substitute pieces W, V, and U for pieces L, K, and J respectively.

2. Create a total of 48 half-square triangles.

3. Use these pieces to create four border sides, with 12 half-square triangles on each side (six facing in one direction and six facing in the opposite direction).

Frame Border X

(See Quilt Layout Diagram)

To create the frame border, sew the Border strips (X) together to make two 1¼" x 58" strips and two 1¼" x 60" strips. Sew the shorter strips to the top and bottom of the quilt top; trim to fit. Then sew the longer strips to the sides; trim to fit.

Frame Border Y

(See Quilt Layout Diagram)

To create the next frame border, sew the Border strips (Y) together to make two 1" x 60" strips and two 1" x 62" strips. Sew the shorter strips to the top and bottom of the quilt top; trim to fit. Then sew the longer strips to the sides; trim to fit.

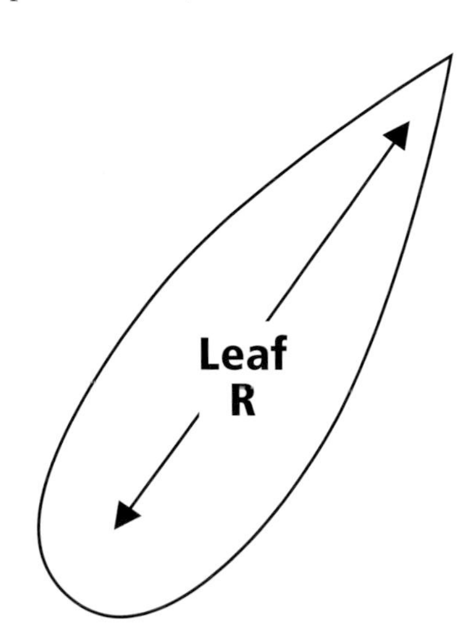

Floral Border

(See Quilt Layout Diagram)

1. To create the floral border, measure the quilt top from top to bottom through the center to obtain the length of the sides.

2. Using Fabric 7, cut two 6½" strips lengthwise, not widthwise (no piecing is necessary by cutting fabric lengthwise). The strips (Z) should be equal to the length you just measured (approximately 53"). Sew these strips to the sides of the quilt.

3. Measure the quilt top from side to side through the center. Cut two 6½" strips lengthwise through the fabric. The strips (Z) should be equal to the width you just measured (approximately 71"). Sew these strips to the top and bottom of the quilt to finish the quilt top.

Quilting and Finishing

(See General Instructions pages 137–141)

1. Layer and baste the quilt top, batting, and backing in preparation for quilting.

2. Hand or machine quilt. This quilt is quilted with a free-form leaf and flower designs and stippling.

3. Finish the quilt by cutting and piecing 2¼" strips of straight-grain binding fabric. Sew binding around quilt using folded mitered corners. ❖

Lisa Quan & Verna Mosquera

LISA QUAN AND VERNA MOSQUERA WERE DRAWN TOGETHER IMMEDIATELY BY their love of quilting. Their get-it-done personalities make their partnership the perfect fit. Both share the dream of inspiring others with their creative ideas. The perfect setting in which to do that is Patchwork Pieces, their pattern company. Here they are both able to design and select color elements.

Lisa Quan (above, left) has been involved in needlework and stitchery since the age of seven. She loved working with her grandmothers on crocheting and embroidery. She has always had a passion for new ideas and designs. During high school she began her first hand piecing, hand quilting class. She has loved quilting ever since. Antique quilts and primitive designs are Lisa's favorites. Moreover, her favorite quilts combine piecing and hand appliqué with new technique ideas. She now enjoys teaching classes in quilting and is also a registered nurse. She and her two daughters and husband live in Castro Valley, California.

Verna Mosquera (above, right) enjoys spending time with her husband and new baby, traveling, and doing anything creative. She started quilting as a New Year's resolution and was hooked from day one. She now devotes endless hours to quilting and is constantly on the hunt for new ideas, which she finds all around her in everyday life. Besides being a partner in Patchwork Pieces, Verna teaches quiltmaking. She gets a great deal of satisfaction seeing people learn as well as sharing in their creative endeavors. Her favorite quilts combine piecing and appliqué, and she considers her strengths to be color and fabric combinations. She feels that the more fabrics there are in her quilts, the better. She plans to quilt forever.

Romantic Baskets

Designed and made by Lisa Quan and Verna Mosquera; quilted by Lynn Todoroff
Finished size: 88"x 107"

This quilt is a blend of patchwork and simple appliqué. It uses many fabrics in numerous floral and woven combinations to give the impression that each individual basket is a quilt in itself. If you do not want to cut all the fabric at once, you can cut the fabric for each size of basket as it is called for in the assembly instructions. Although making this quilt requires time and patience, it is sure to become a favorite in your personal collection.

Materials

Yardage (based on 45" fabric, from selvage to selvage)

Fabric 1: ½ yd. each of 25 assorted light prints
Fabric 2: ⅜ yd. each of 50 assorted medium to dark prints
Fabric 3: ¼ yd. each of 30 assorted checks and stripes
Fabric 4: 1⅞ yds. light green stripes
Fabric 5: ¼ yd. rose print
Fabric 6: 1⅝ yds. light rose print
Fabric 7: 1⅛ yds. green floral print
Batting: King-size, or 5½ yds.
Backing: 7¾ yds.
Binding: ¾ yds.
Freezer paper
#10 straw needles
Appliqué thread to match basket handles
Bias bars in ¾", ½", and ⅜" widths

Cutting

(See Quilt Layout Diagram)
Cut all fabric crosswise, from selvage to selvage, unless otherwise instructed.

12-inch Basket Block

(Fig. 1. Make 12 blocks.)

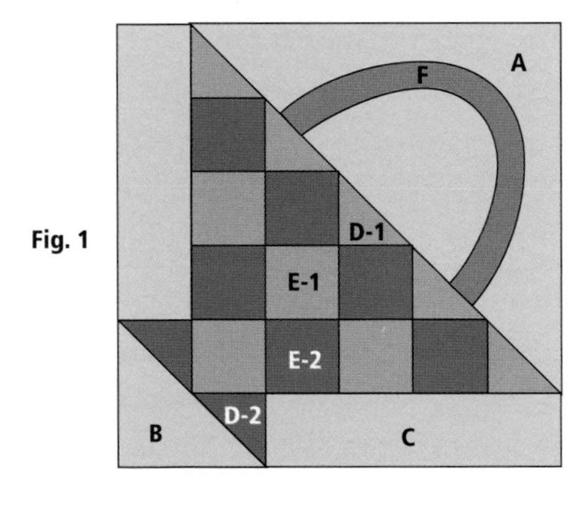

Fig. 1

FABRIC 1

Choose six background fabrics. Use each to cut fabric for two baskets:

PIECE A: Cut one 10⅞" square; cut on the diagonal to create two triangles.

PIECE B: Cut one 4⅞" square; cut on the diagonal to create two triangles.

PIECE C: Cut four 2½" x 8½" rectangles.

FABRIC 2

Choose 24 basket fabrics; use two contrasting fabrics in each basket:

PIECE D-1: From one fabric, cut three 2⅞" squares; cut on the diagonal to create six triangles. Discard one triangle; only five are needed.

PIECE D-2: From contrasting fabric, cut one 2⅞" square; cut square in half on the diagonal to create two triangles.

PIECE E: Cut two 2½" x 10½" strips—one from each of the contrasting fabrics (E-1 and E-2).

Romantic Baskets Quilt Layout

- Fabric 1 - assorted light prints
- Fabric 2 - assorted medium to dark prints
- Fabric 3 - assorted checks and stripes
- Fabric 4 - light green stripes
- Fabric 5 - rose print
- Fabric 6 - light rose print
- Fabric 7 - green floral print

FABRIC 3

Choose 12 assorted fabrics for the 12-inch basket handles. From each of the 12 handle fabrics:

PIECE F: Cut one 10" square. Cut one 2" strip from the widest part of the diagonal (Fig. 2) to create a bias strip. Save the resulting triangles for the smaller basket handles.

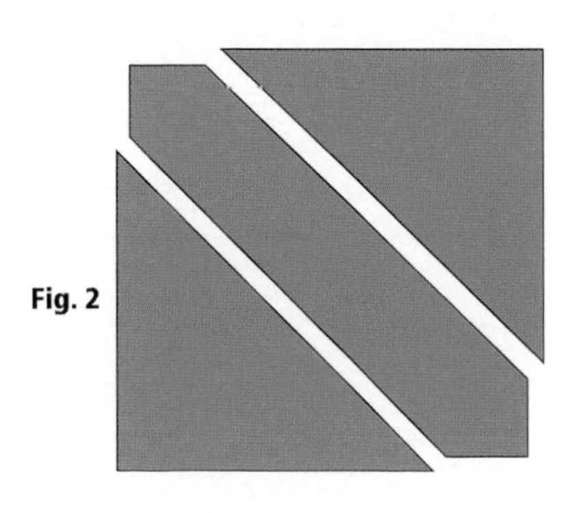

Fig. 2

6-inch Basket Blocks

(Fig. 3. Make 40 blocks.)

Fig. 3

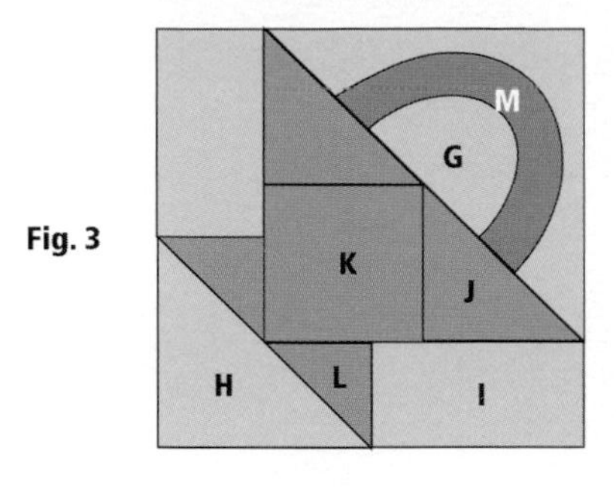

FABRIC 1

Choose ten background fabrics. Use each to cut fabric for four blocks.

PIECE G: Cut two 5⅜" squares, and then cut each square in half on the diagonal to create four triangles.

PIECE H: Cut two 3⅞" squares, and then cut on the diagonal to create four triangles.

PIECE I: Cut eight 2" x 3½" rectangles.

FABRIC 2

Choose 20 basket fabrics; use two contrasting fabrics in each basket.

PIECE J: From one fabric, cut four 3⅛" squares, and then cut each square in half on the diagonal to create eight triangles.

PIECE L: From the same fabric, cut four 2⅜" squares, and then cut each square in half on the diagonal to create eight triangles.

PIECE K: From contrasting fabric, cut four 2¾" squares.

FABRIC 3

PIECE M: Using remaining handle fabrics and 12" basket handle scraps, cut one 5" square. Turn on point and cut one 1⅜" strip from the widest part of the diagonal to create a bias strip (see Fig. 2).

4-inch Basket Blocks

(Fig. 4. Make 50 blocks.)

Fig. 4

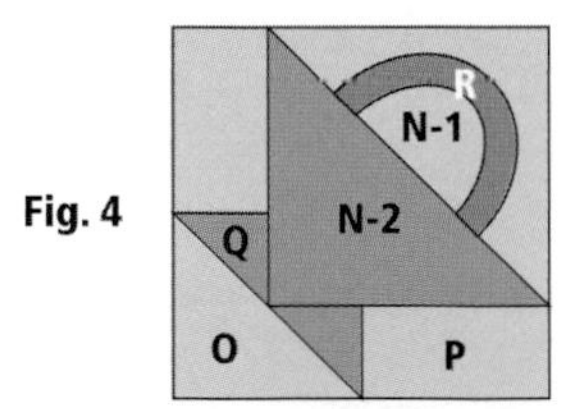

FABRIC 1

Choose 25 background fabrics. Use each to cut fabric for two blocks.

PIECE N-1: Cut one 3⅞" square, and then cut the square in half on the diagonal to create two triangles.
PIECE O: Cut one 2⅞" square, and then cut on the diagonal to create two triangles.
PIECE P: Cut four 1½" x 2½" rectangles.

FABRIC 2
Choose 25 background fabrics. Use each to cut fabric for two blocks.
PIECE N-2: Cut one 3⅞" squares, and then cut each square in half on the diagonal to create two triangles.
PIECE Q: Cut two 1⅞" squares, and then cut the squares in half on the diagonal to create four triangles.

FABRIC 3
PIECE R: Using remaining handle fabric and handle scraps, cut one 4" square. Turn on point and cut one 1⅛" strip from the widest part of the diagonal to create a bias strip (see Fig. 2).

Nine Patch

FABRIC 1
PIECE S: Using 20 fabrics, cut (40) 4½" squares.

Sashing and Posts

FABRIC 4
PIECE T: Cut (26) 2¼" strips. Then cut these strips into (80) 2¼" x 12½" strips.

FABRIC 5
FOR PIECE U: Cut two 2¼" strips. Then cut these strips into (31) 2¼" squares.

Setting and Corner Triangles

FABRIC 6
PIECE V: Cut seven 21¼" squares, and then cut each square in half on both diagonals to create the (14) setting triangles.
PIECE W: Cut two 13⅞" squares, and then cut each square in half on one diagonal to create the four corner triangles.

Border

FABRIC 7
PIECES X AND Y: Cut nine 4¼" strips.

Binding

Cut ten 2⅛" strips.

Romantic Baskets by Lisa Quan and Verna Mosquera

Construction

All seams are ¼" unless otherwise noted. Sew with right sides together.

12-inch Basket Block

Finished size: 12" x 12"
(See Fig. 1. Make 12 blocks.)

To make each basket handle:

1. Fold the bias strip (F) in half, wrong sides together, along the long edge. Do not press. Sew the strip closed using a ⅛" seam allowance.

2. Slide a ¾" bias bar through the sewn tube. Turn the sewn tube until the seam is centered down one side of the bias bar. With bar inside, press both sides, pressing the seam to one side.

3. Carefully remove the (hot) bar and press fabric flat.

To appliqué each basket handle (F) to piece (A):

4. To maintain uniformity among the baskets, mark the placement of each handle consistently, using a freezer paper template. To make the template cut out a 10½" square of freezer paper. Cut the square in half on the diagonal to create two triangles. Fold one paper triangle in half to make a center line. Measure down 3" from the top point and 4" from one side along the bottom and mark with dots (Fig. 5).

5. With a pencil, draw a curve that joins the dots; fold the paper in half and trace over the first curve to create an identical curve

on other side of the triangle. Trace over this line on the front of your freezer paper to create a continuous arc. Now trace a second curve ½" below the first following the same procedure (Fig. 5). Trace handle shape onto (12) fabric pieces (A).

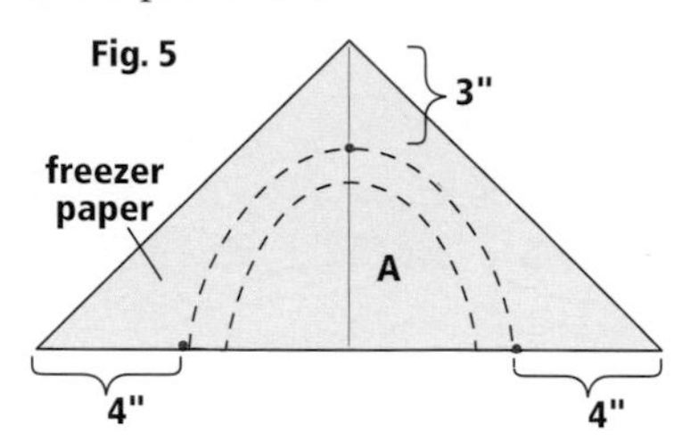

6. Hand baste handle to background, covering placement line. Appliqué the handle (see General Instructions, Freezer Paper Appliqué, Steps 5 and 6, on page 135).

To piece the base of each basket:

7. Sew a 2½" x 10½" strip (E-1) from the first fabric to a 2½" x 10½" strip (E-2) from the second fabric, along the 10½" side to create a strip set. Press seam toward the first fabric.

8. Cut the strip set into four 2½" units (Fig. 6). Each unit will have one E-1 square and one E-2 square.

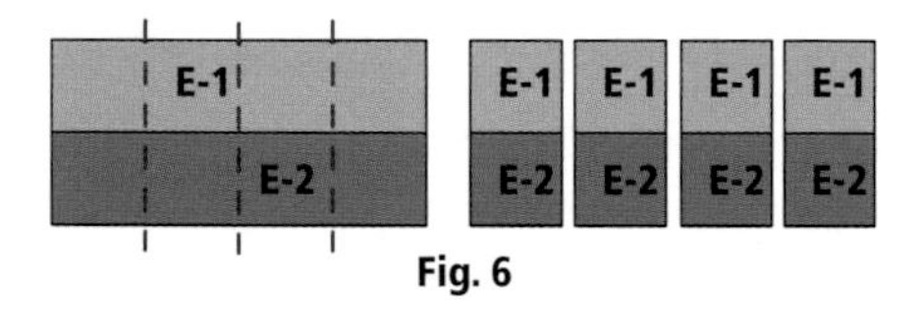

Fig. 6

9. To create the basket bottom, sew the pieces in rows (Fig. 7), pressing the seams toward lighter color:

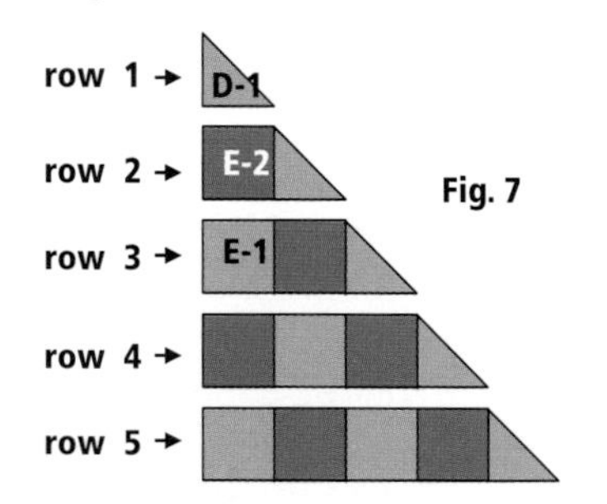

10. Sew together Rows 1–5. Press all the seams in one direction.

11. Sew each Piece C to a D-2 piece. Press the seams toward C.

12. Refer to Fig. 8. Sew C/D units to sides of the basket. Sew B to the basket base. Press seams in direction of arrows.

13. Find the center of both the basket base and the basket handle unit by folding each piece in half and finger pressing a center point. Line up the two pieces at their center point, pin, and sew. Press the seams toward the handle unit (Fig. 8).

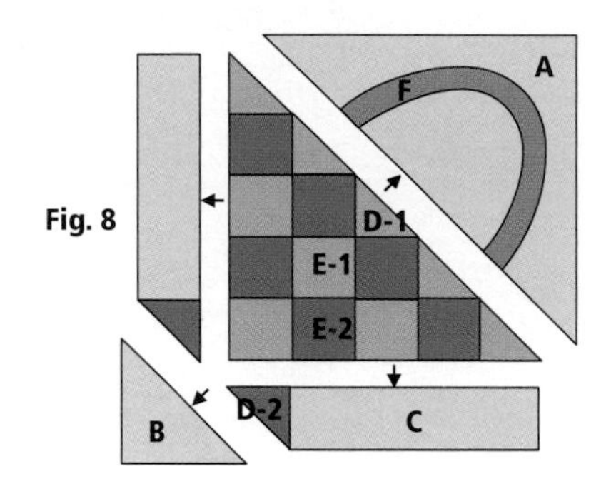

14. Square up the block, trimming if necessary, so that it measures 12½" square.

6-inch Basket Block

Finished size: 6" x 6"

(See Fig. 3. Make 40 blocks.)

To make each basket handle:

1. Follow the instructions for making the 12-inch basket handles, Steps 1–3, except use a ½" bias bar and pieces G and M.

2. Follow instructions for appliquéing 12" basket handles, Steps 4–6, except cut a 5⅜" square of freezer paper and adjust measurements on Fig. 5 as follows: Measure down 2¼" from the point and 2⅞" in from one side on the bottom. Draw a curve ⅜" below the first.

To piece the base of each basket:

3. Refer to Fig. 9. Sew both J pieces to Piece K. Press seams toward K. Sew Pieces I to L. Press the seam toward L.

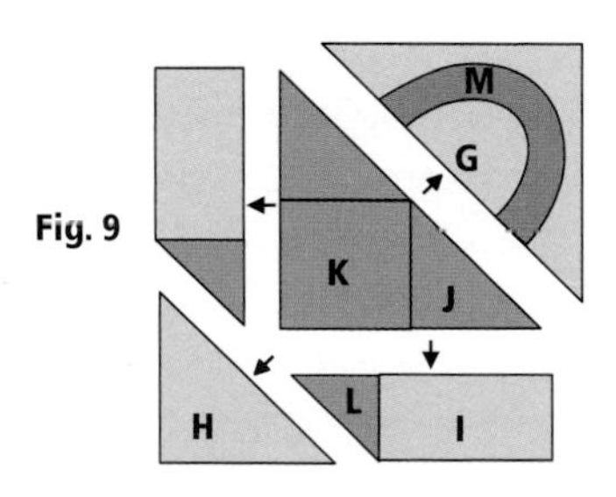

4. Sew L/I units to sides of basket. Sew H to basket bases. Press seams in direction of arrows.

5. Follow instructions for the 12-inch basket block, Steps 13–14, except square the block to 6½" and refer to Fig. 3.

4-inch Basket Block

Finished size: 4" x 4"

(See Fig. 4. Make 50 blocks.)

To make each basket handle:

1. Follow instructions for the 12-inch basket handles, Steps 1–3, except use a ⅜" bias bar and pieces N1 and R.

2. Follow the instructions for appliquéing 12" basket handles, Steps 4–6, except cut a 3⅞" square of freezer paper and adjust measurements on Fig. 5 as follows: Measure down 1¼" from the top point and 2" in from one side on the bottom. Draw a curve ¼" below the first.

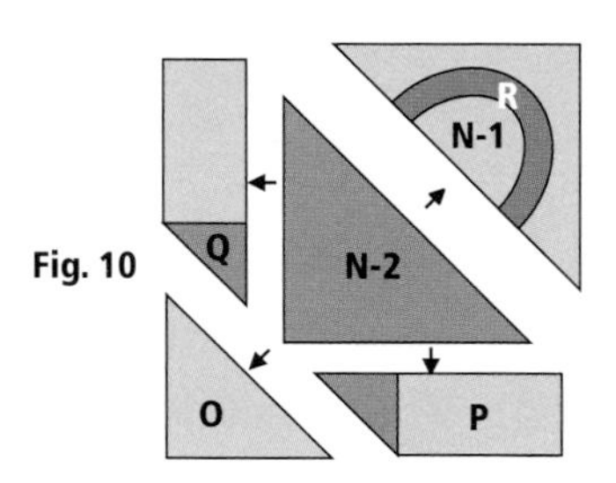

To piece the base of each basket:

3. Refer to Fig. 10. Sew Pieces P to Q. Press seams toward P.

4. Sew P/Q units to Piece N-2. Sew O to basket bases. Press seams in direction of arrows.

5. Follow instructions for the 12-inch basket block, Steps 13–14, except square the block to 4½" and refer to Fig. 4.

Assembly

Patch Blocks

1. Use the (40) 6-inch baskets to make ten four-patch blocks. All four handles should face center (Fig. 11). Sew blocks into rows, then sew rows together. Press seams in direction of arrows.

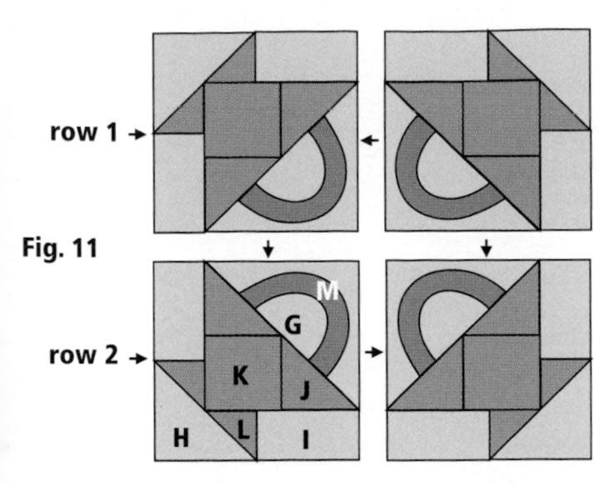

Fig. 11

2. Sew five 4-inch basket blocks and four S pieces into nine-patch blocks, with the basket handles facing up (Fig. 12). Sew blocks into rows, then sew rows together. Press seams in direction of arrows. Repeat for a total of ten nine-patch blocks.

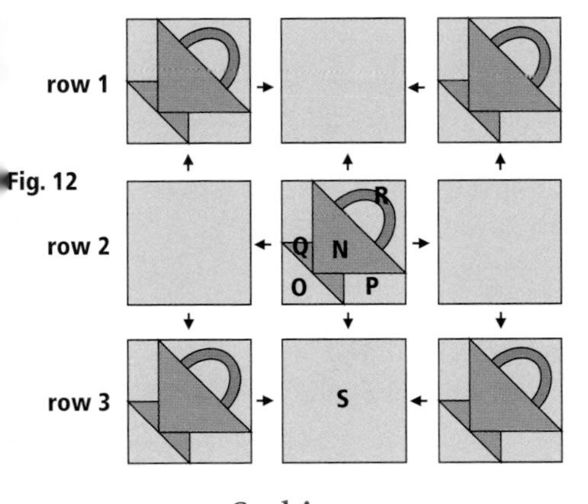

Fig. 12

Sashing

3. Lay out the blocks in diagonal rows, starting with the upper right block as Row 1 as shown in Quilt Layout Diagram on page 66 and Fig. 13.

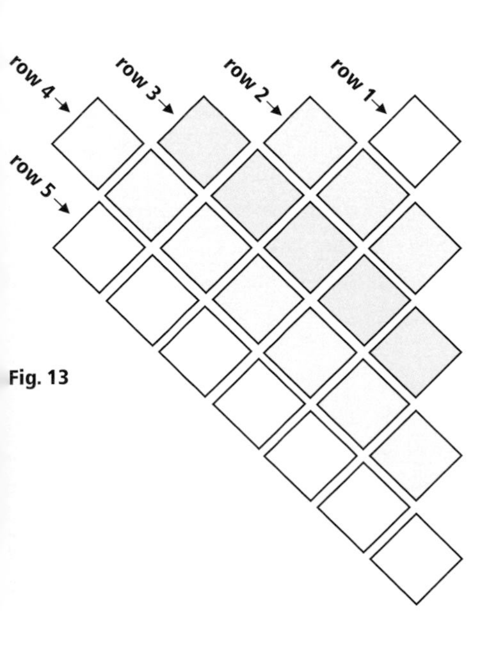

Fig. 13

4. Sew the blocks into rows with sashing (T) in between each block and on the ends of each row (Fig. 14). You will have a total of eight block rows. Press the seams toward the sashing.

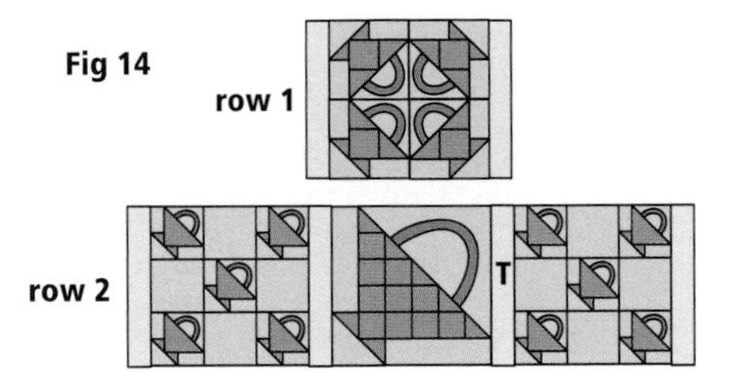

Fig 14

5. Using the Quilt Layout Diagram as a guide for length of rows, join the remaining sashing pieces (T) into rows with posts (U) in between and at the ends of each sashing strip (Fig. 15). You will have a total of nine sashing rows. Press the seams toward the sashing.

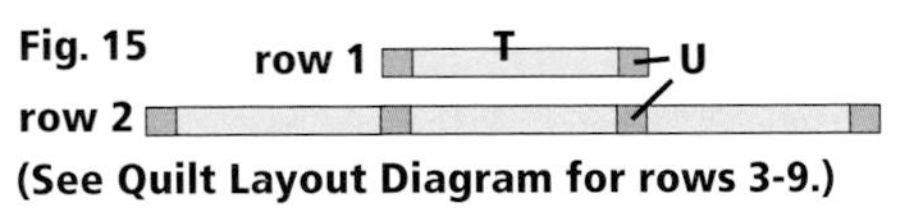

Fig. 15

(See Quilt Layout Diagram for rows 3-9.)

6. Starting from the top right corner of the quilt, sew a sashing row to the top of Rows 1 through 4, being careful to line up posts and sashes (Fig. 16).

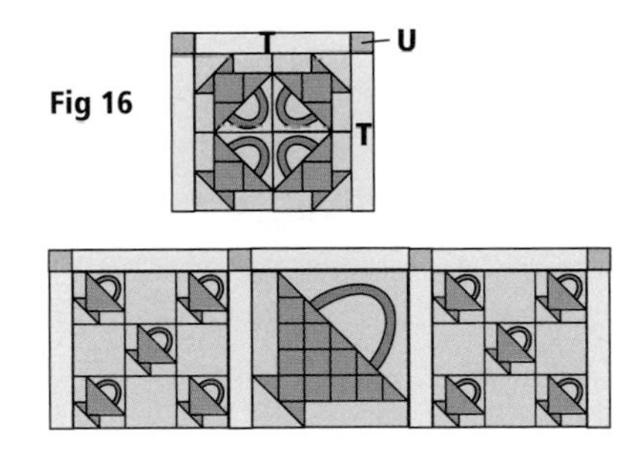

Fig 16

7. Leave the fifth sashing row loose for now, do not attach it to anything.

8. Sew a sashing row to the bottom of Rows 5–8.

Setting and Corner Triangles

9. Starting from the top right corner of the quilt, add a setting triangle (V) to both sides of Rows 1, 2, and 3 (Fig. 17).

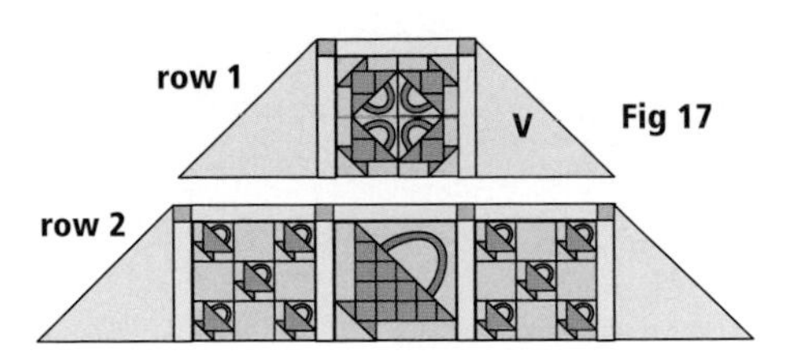

Fig 17

10. Add a setting triangle (V) to Row 4 on the right side only and to Row 5 on the left side only. Remember to reverse the direction of the triangle (see Quilt Layout Diagram).

11. Add a setting triangle (V) to both sides of Rows 6, 7, and 8. Remember to reverse the direction of the triangles.

12. Sew all of the rows together, attaching the remaining sashing row to the bottom of Row 4 and the top of Row 5.

13. Add a corner triangle (W) to each corner of the quilt.

14. Square up edges of quilt on all four sides.

Border

15. Join two 4¼" strips (X) together; repeat. Sew these strips to the top and bottom of the quilt. Trim as necessary to fit the quilt.

16. Join two strips plus one 21" strip, and repeat to create sides of quilt. Sew to the sides, and trim as necessary to complete the quilt top.

Quilting and Finishing

(See General Instructions pages 137–141)

1. Layer and baste together the quilt top, batting, and backing in preparation for quilting.

2. Hand or machine quilt. I machine-quilted my baskets in small squares and used large flowers in the setting triangles. I machine-stippled the backgrounds of the basket blocks.

3. Finish the quilt by cutting and piecing 2¼" strips of straight-grain binding fabric. Sew binding around quilt using folded mitered corners. ❖

Floral Romance

Designed, made, and quilted by Lisa Quan and Verna Mosquera
Finished size: 54" x 54"

The inspiration for this quilt came from wanting to design something that looks complex but is actually very simple. The subtle rose and green florals in this quilt lend a romantic quality that is enhanced by choosing soft, coordinating prints for the pieced blocks. The detail in the floral blocks adds texture and interest to the pattern. You can use this design to create a different effect by working within one fabric line, combining fabric lines, using all plaids, or using novelty prints for the pieced blocks and then complementing them with a different novelty print in the alternate blocks.

Materials

Yardage (based on 42" fabric, from selvage to selvage)

Fabric 1: 1¾ yds. each of 28 light to dark assorted prints
Fabric 2: 2½ yds. large floral
Fabric 3: ⅝ yd. medium floral
Fabric 4*: ¾ yd. red plaid
Backing: 3½ yds.
Batting: 2 yds. (60" wide)

*We used the same fabric for the first border and binding. If you want to use a different fabric for the binding, buy ⅓ yd. of Fabric 4 and ⅜ yd. of binding fabric.)

Cutting

(See Quilt Layout Diagram)
Cut all fabric crosswise, from selvage to selvage, unless otherwise instructed.

Pieced Square Block

(Fig. 1)

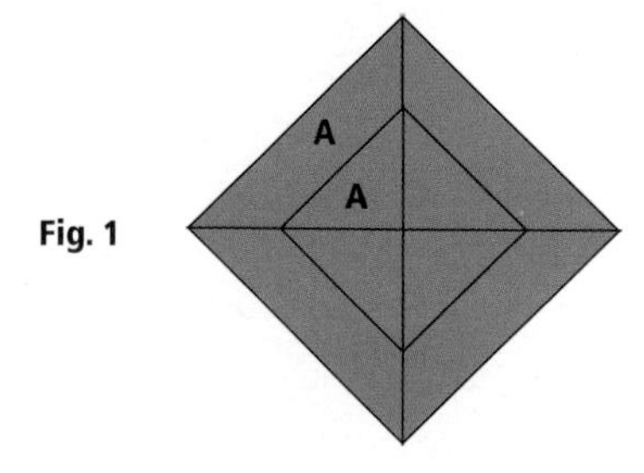

Fig. 1

FABRIC 1

PIECE A: From each of the assorted fabrics, cut one 2" strip the width of the fabric for a total of 28 strips. Then, cut each 2" strip in half.

Alternate Blocks

FABRIC 2

PIECE B: Cut six 5¾" strips from the large floral fabric. Then cut these strips into 5¾" squares for a total of 36 squares.

Setting and Corner Triangles

FABRIC 3

PIECE C: Cut two 8¾" strips. Then cut these strips into six 8¾" squares. Cut each square twice on the diagonal (each square yields four triangles) for a total of 24 setting triangles.

PIECE D: Cut two 4¾" squares. Cut each square once on the diagonal for a total of four corner triangles.

Borders and Binding

FABRIC 4

PIECE E: Cut six 2" strips.

FABRIC 2

PIECE F: Cut the fabric in half lengthwise to create a 22" x 54" piece. From the 22" x 54" piece, cut four 4" x 54" strips on the lengthwise grain.

For the binding

From the remaining portion of the 22" x 54" piece (or your alternate binding fabric), cut two 2⅛" x 54" strips on the lengthwise grain and three 2⅛" x 45" strips for a total of five binding strips.

Construction

All seams should be ¼" unless otherwise noted. Sew with right sides together.

Pieced Squares

Finished size: 5¼" x 5¼"
(See Fig. 1. Make 25 blocks.)

To make each pieced-square block:

1. Sew together two 2" x 22" assorted strips (A) down their longest side, varying colors; press.

2. Make a template from template A on page 73 (see General Instructions page 132). Use this template to cut triangles out of the sewn strips (Fig. 2).

NOTE: The tip of the fabric may not quite reach the edge of the template. It is okay if the tip of the triangle is cut off.

3. Sew four triangles together to make a square (Fig. 3).

4. Trim all four sides of the block until the block measures 5¾" square.

Assembly

1. Lay out the alternate (B) and pieced-square blocks (A) in diagonal rows (Fig. 4), always starting and ending with an alternate block.

2. Sew the blocks together to make Rows 1–9, and then press the seams in the direction of the alternate blocks (B).

3. Sew a side triangle (C) to both ends of Rows 1–4 and 6–9. **NOTE:** The setting and corner triangles are cut oversized to allow quilt edges to be trimmed after assembly.

4. Sew corner triangles (D) to ends of Row 5.

5. Sew side triangles (C) to both ends of two remaining alternate blocks (B). Sew a corner triangle (D) to outside corners of the two alternate blocks (B) and press (Fig. 5).

6. Sew together corner units and rows; press.

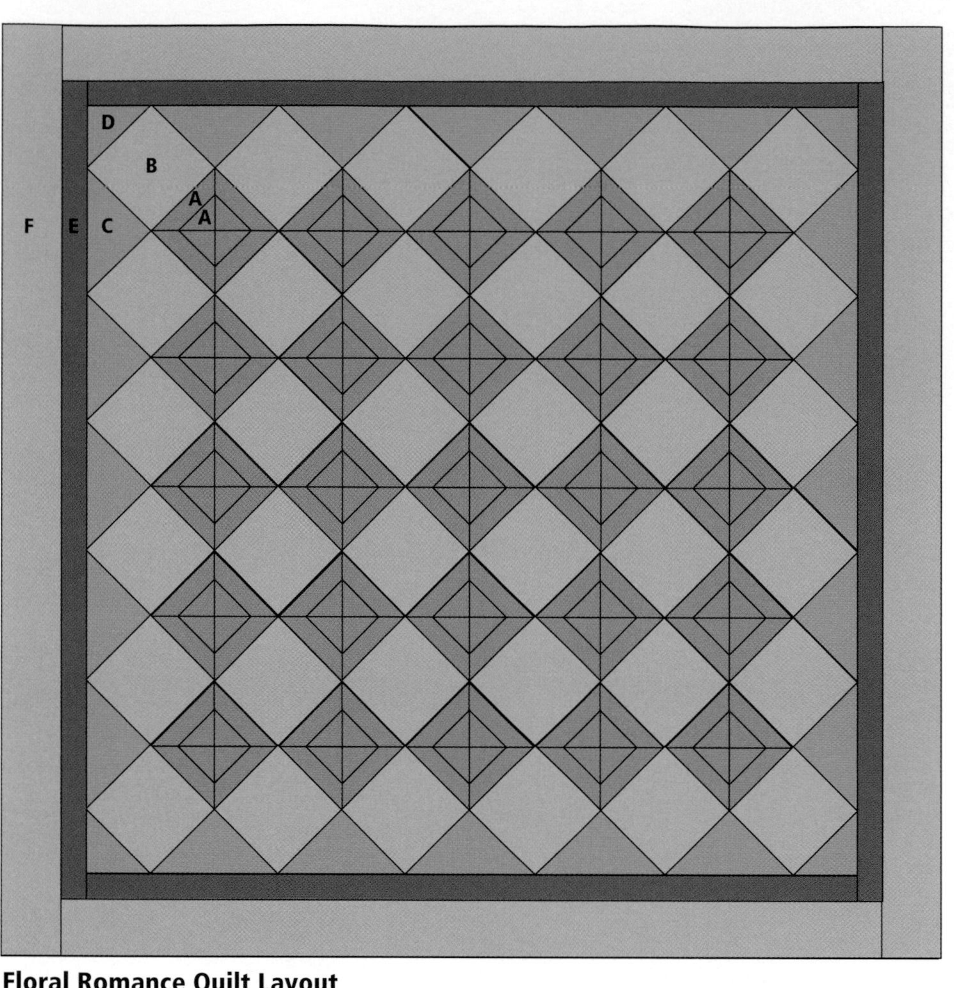

Floral Romance Quilt Layout

Fabric 1 - 28 light-to-dark assorted prints

Fabric 2 - large floral

Fabric 3 - medium floral

Fabric 4 -red plaid

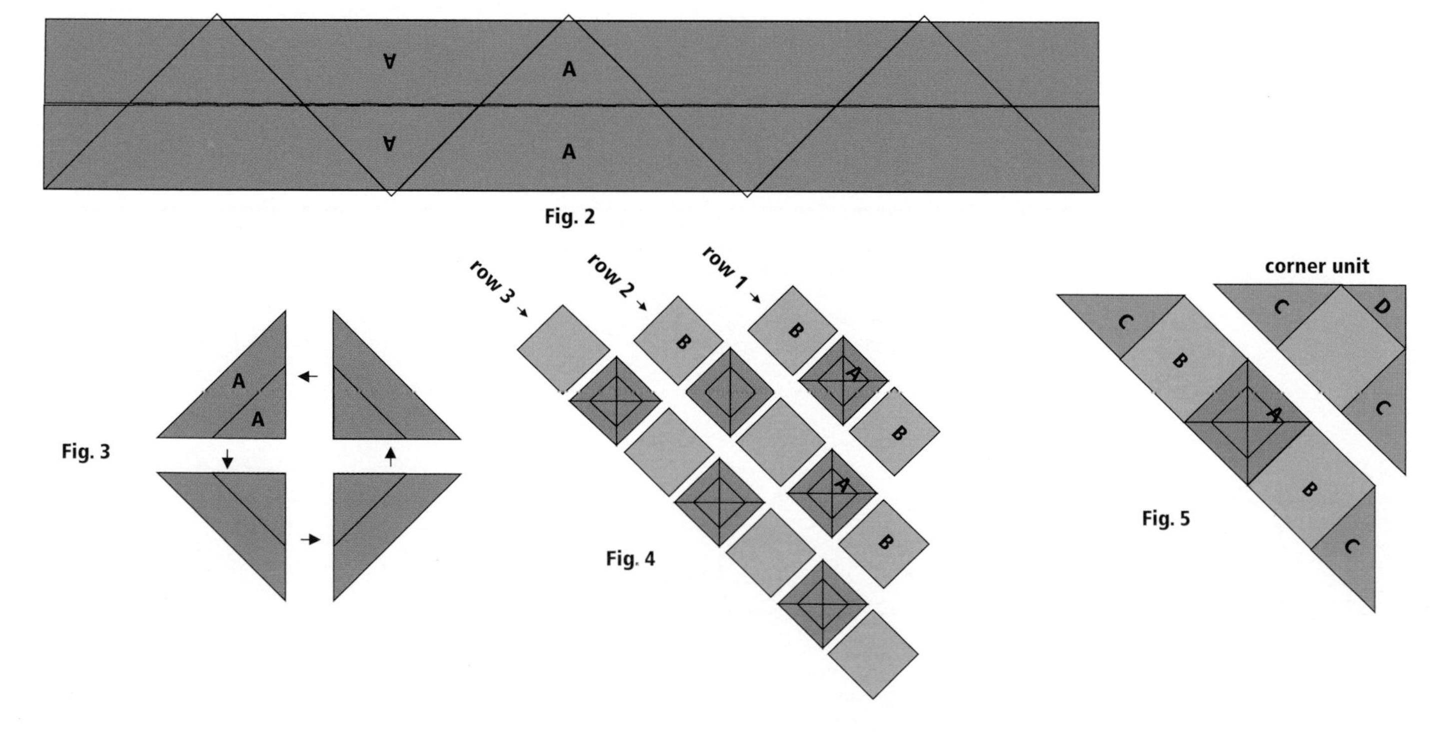

Fig. 2

Fig. 3

Fig. 4

Fig. 5

Borders and Binding

(Fig. 6)

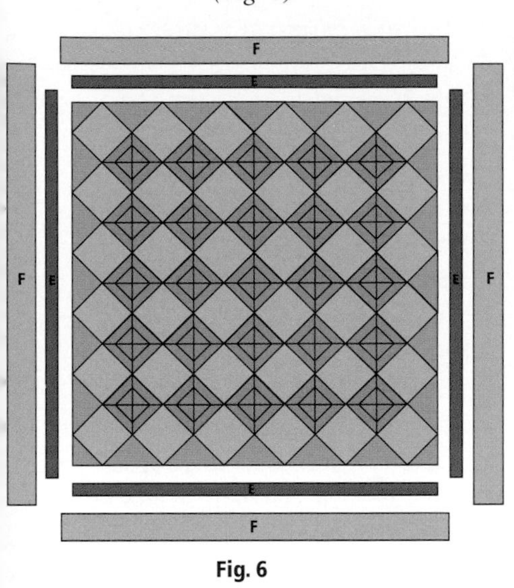

Fig. 6

7. To create first border, cut two strips in half. Sew a half strip to each of the remaining strips.

8. Sew a strip to the top and bottom sides of quilt; press and trim to fit.

9. Sew a strip to each side of quilt; press and trim to fit.

10. to create the second border, sew the second border strips (F) to the top and bottom of the quilt top; press and trim to fit. Sew the remaining border strips (F) to the sides of the quilt top; press and trim to fit to complete the quilt top.

Quilting and Finishing

(See General Instructions pages 137–141)

1. Layer and baste together the quilt top, batting, and backing in preparation for quilting.

Floral Romance by Lisa Quan and Verna Mosquera

2. Hand or machine quilt. For this quilt, we stippled by machine.

3. Finish the quilt by cutting and piecing 2¼" strips of straight-grain binding fabric. Sew binding around quilt using folded mitered corners. ❖

align strip seam line here

Template A

Gardening Angel Pillow

Designed, made, and quilted by Lisa Quan and Verna Mosquera
Finished size: 22" x 22"

We designed this pillow to blend simple patchwork and appliqué. Once we had our design, we went through our scraps to see what worked well together. We used the large floral fabric in the wing to establish our color theme, and then combined this with matching stripes, plaids, and geometric prints. Another approach would be to combine floral prints for the angel, and then use geometric prints in the background and border. We finished the pillow by attaching binding around the edges to give it a cording effect.

Materials

Yardage (based on 42" fabric from selvage to selvage)

Fabric 1: ¼ yd. light cream
Fabric 2: ⅓ yd. gold check
Fabric 3: ⅛ yd. medium cream
Fabric 4: ⅛ yd. gold with stripes
Fabric 5: ⅛ yd. gold print
Fabric 6: 6" x 10" piece pink
Fabric 7: ¼ yd. red plaid
Fabric 8: 6" x 8" piece green stripe
Fabric 9: 6" x 8" piece floral
Fabric 10: 10" square green print
Fabric 11: ⅛ yd. assorted scraps
Fabric 12: ¼ yd. red with stripes
Backing: ½ yd.
Binding: ¼ yd.
Batting: 21½" square of thin batting
22" pillow (or ⅝ yd. muslin and one bag of stuffing)
⅜" bias bar
Embroidery floss for face and herringbone stitch

Cutting

(See Gardening Angel Layout Diagram)

Background

FABRIC 1
PIECE A: Cut one 7½" x 12½" rectangle.

FABRIC 2
PIECE B: Cut one 9½" x 12½" rectangle.

FABRIC 3
PIECE C: Cut one 4½" x 9½" rectangle.

FABRIC 4
PIECE D: Cut one 3½" x 4½" rectangle.

FABRIC 5
PIECE E: Cut one 4½" square.

Angel's Body

Trace full-size Templates F – S onto freezer paper (see General Instructions, page 135, for freezer paper method).

FABRIC 6
Use Templates F, G, H, and I to cut out the angel's face, hand, and feet.

FABRIC 7
Use Template J to cut out the angel's dress.

FABRIC 8
Use Templates K, L, and M to cut out the angel's arm and legs.

FABRIC 9
Use Template N to cut out the angel's wing.

Flower Vine

FABRIC 10
PIECE O: Cut three 1⅛" strips on the bias.

FABRIC 11
Use Template P to cut out the angel's halo.
Use Template Q, to cut out five stars.
Use Template R to cut out seven leaves
Use Template S to cut out three tulips.

Border, Backing, and Binding

FABRIC 12
For Piece T: Cut two 3" strips.

BACKING
Cut one 14¼" x 21½" piece.
Cut one 12½" x 21½" piece.

BINDING
Cut three 2¼" strips.

PILLOW INSERT (OPTIONAL)
Cut two 22" squares of muslin.

Construction

(Fig. 1)

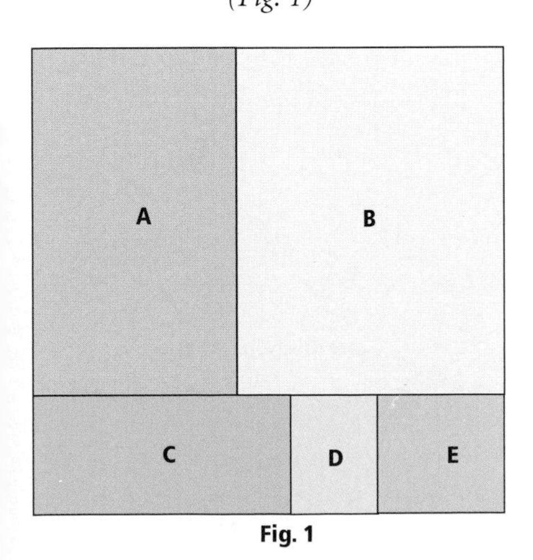

Fig. 1

1. Sew together background pieces A and B along the 12½" side to form the top of the background (Fig. 2).

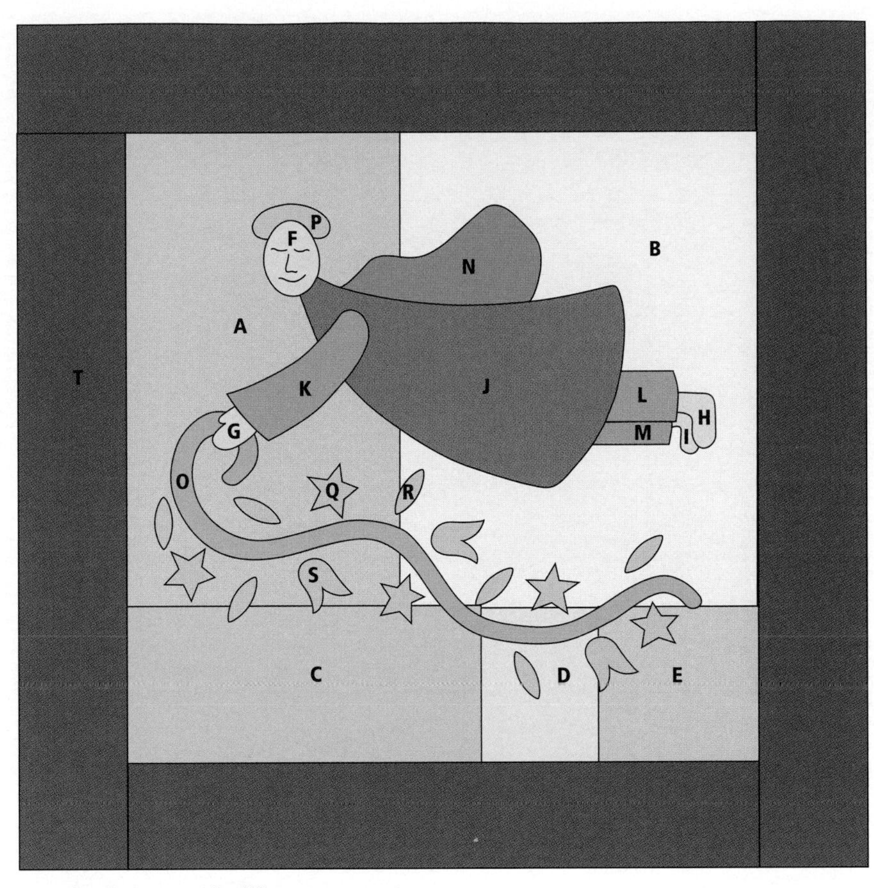

Gardening Angel Pillow Layout

2. Sew together background pieces C, D, and E along the 4½" side to form the bottom part of the background (Fig. 2).

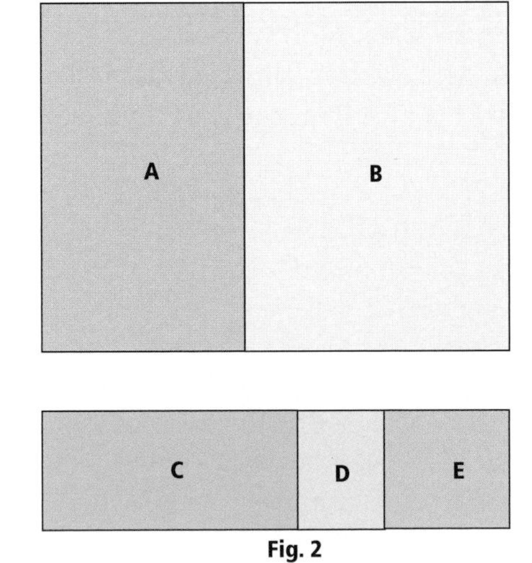

Fig. 2

3. Sew the top of the background to the bottom of the background along the longest side.

Gardening Angel Pillow by Lisa Quan and Verna Mosquera

Assembly

(Fig. 3)

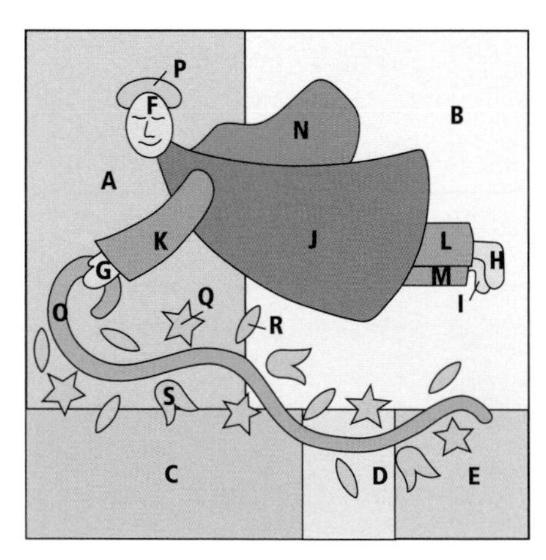

Fig. 3

1. To prepare applique pieces see the General Instructions, Freezer Paper Appliqué, on page 135.

2. To prepare the vine, sew together the bias strips on the diagonal, and then press the seams in one direction. Sew the strip, wrong sides together, using a ⅛" seam allowance. Slide the bias bar through, center the seam, and then press the vine flat. Remove the bias bar, being careful not to touch it, as ironing can make it very hot.

3. Enlarge the design layout (Fig. 5 on page 78) and transfer the drawing to the right side of your pieced background with a pencil or washable marker.

4. Center bias vine over line on the background, and then baste it in place. Then, lay out the angel, flowers, leaves, and stars. Using your favorite appliqué method (see General Instructions, pages 134–135), appliqué all these pieces to the background.

5. Square up the edges of the background to make sure they are even.

6. Attach border (T) to angel center using a log cabin style. Sew and trim Border strip (T) to fit in the order shown in (Fig. 4).

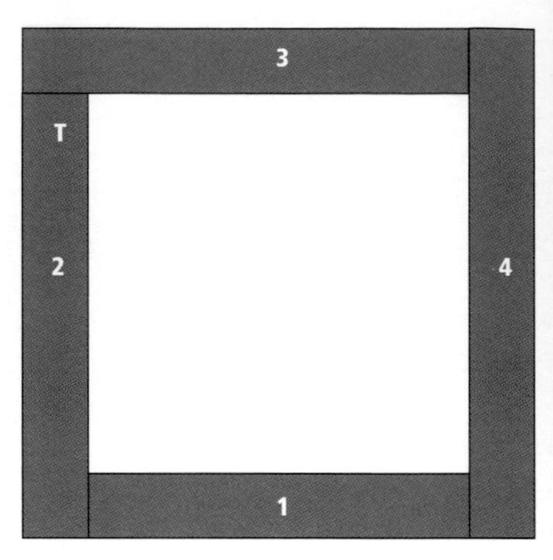

Fig. 4

Quilting and Finishing

(See General Instructions pages 137–141)

1. Quilt the top as desired. To add detail to the pillow, we used a backstitch (Fig. 6) to create the angel's face. We used a herringbone stitch (Fig. 7) where the background meets the borders of the pillow.

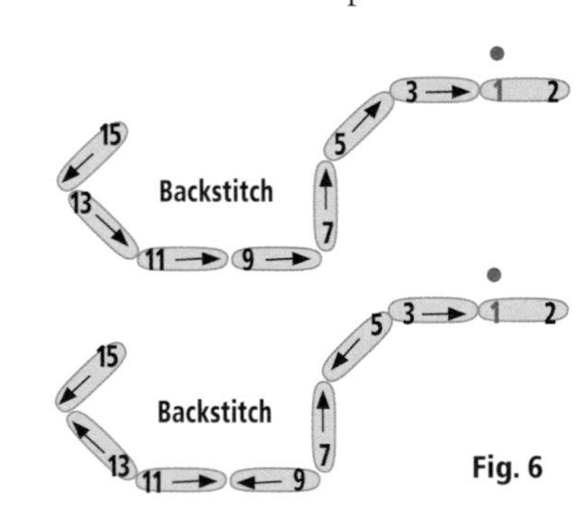

Fig. 6

Fig. 7

2. Center pieced pillow top over a square of 21½" batting. Baste ¼" in from outside edge of pillow.

3. I machined quilted around appliqué shapes and stippled the background.

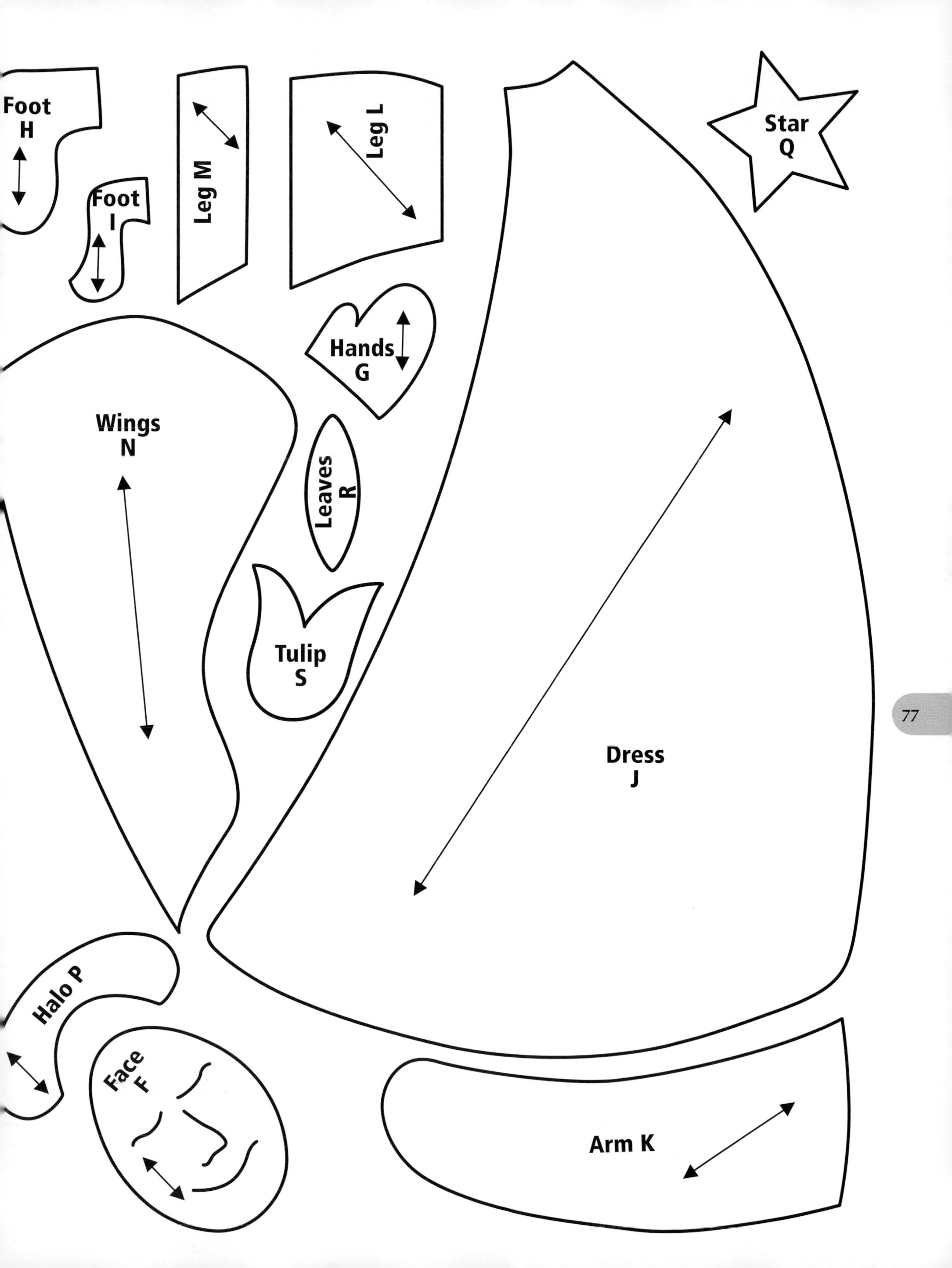

Foot
H
Foot
I
Leg M
Leg L
Star
Q
Hands
G
Wings
N
Leaves
R
Tulip
S
Dress
J
Halo P
Face
F
Arm K

4. Square up the edges of the pillow front, to prepare to construct the pillow back.

5. For each pillow backing piece, turn the fabric under ½" on the 20½" side, and then turn it under another ½" and stitch a hem.

6. Place pillow top wrong side up on a flat surface. Over this place the two backing pieces right side up, overlapping each other in the center. Adjust backing overlap until pillow top and backing edges are even.

7. Pin backing overlap closed and machine baste the two layers together ¼" in from outside edges to avoid shifting while binding.

8. Sew together the three 2¼" binding strips.

9. Attach the binding to pillow edge following General Instructions for folded mitered corner on pages 140–141.

10. To make the pillow insert (if you did not buy a pillow), sew together the two 22" x 22" pieces of muslin, with wrong sides together, using a ½" seam allowance. Leave an opening for turning the pieces. Clip the corners, turn, and stuff. Whipstitch the opening to close it.

11. Remove pins from the pillow backing and insert the pillow form into the pillow. ❖

Appliqué Layout **1 square = 1**

Enlarge Angel layout with graph paper by plotting points on the grid and joining points.
Enlarge Angel layout with a scanner or enlarging copier set at 200%.

Fig. 5

Sandy Newman

I WAS BORN AND BRED IN NEW ZEALAND AND QUILTING WAS NOT COMMON WHILE I WAS growing up, although I remember the Grandmother's Flower Garden pillows that my mother would hand piece in the summertime at the beach house.

The first quilt I made was during the year that I spent here in the United States going to school. I made it for my boyfriend who was leaving for college. I still have that quilt, as that boyfriend is now my husband.

I didn't start quilting seriously again until about 11 years ago when I was pregnant with our daughter. I was taught to quilt by a friend who had a Monday night sewing class at her house. After that first completed project I was hooked and quilted as much as time would allow.

My favorite quilts to make are baby quilts or wall hangings because they are quick to piece, they can be machine quilted on the sewing machine without too much effort, they make wonderful gifts, and they can be used to decorate walls or as table toppers. Along with my quilting projects, there is often a sweater waiting in the knitting basket to be finished, and I usually have a piece of embroidery or cross stitch that I work on while I sit at sport practice or wait to collect the children from school.

I have been a member of the staff at ThimbleCreek for six years now, and I get just as excited and inspired by the new lines of fabric arriving at the store as I did when I first started.

Hearts

Designed and made by Sandy Newman; quilted by Sandy Klop
Finished size: 40" x 54"

The joy of this quilt is that it is so fast and easy to put together. I designed it for ThimbleCreek as a crib quilt, but a larger version would make a wonderful Valentine's Day gift. Although I have chosen traditional red hearts, you might want to experiment with some other color. Whatever your choice, remember that what lends this quilt a cheerful tone is its simplicity, both in design and color combinations. Although the red hearts and dark blue border provide contrast and energy to the quilt, both pick up colors in the floral background and the small print used behind each heart to create a sense of harmony.

Materials

Yardage (based on 42" fabric, from selvage to selvage)

Fabric 1*: 2¼ yds. yellow floral
Fabric 2: ¾ yd. yellow print
Fabric 3: 1 yd. red
Fabric 4: ¼ yd. blue
Batting: 45" x 60" crib batting
Backing: 1⅝ yds.
Fusible web: 1½ yds.
Thread to match heart fabric

** This quilt uses the same fabric for the outside border and binding. If you use a different fabric for the binding, deduct ½ yd. from Fabric 1. The total yardage for binding should be ½ yd.*

Cutting

(See Quilt Layout Diagram)
Cut all fabric crosswise, from selvage to selvage, unless otherwise instructed.

FABRIC 1

Piece C: Cut (24) 4½" x 6½" rectangles.
Piece F: Cut two 5½" strips.
Piece G: Cut three 5½" strips.

FABRIC 2

Piece B: Cut (25) 4½" x 6½" rectangles.

FABRIC 3

Piece A: Make a template* using Heart A on page 83 (see General Instructions, Machine Appliqué, page 134). Trace 25* heart shapes onto the fusible web. Follow the manufacturer's instructions to fuse the web to the fabric. Cut out the hearts (A). *
Note: In the quilt shown, the template was reversed when tracing 13 of the hearts to create a subtle variation in the design.

FABRIC 4

Piece D: Cut two 1½" strips for the top and bottom of the border.
Piece E: Cut three 1½" x 44½" strips for the sides of the border.

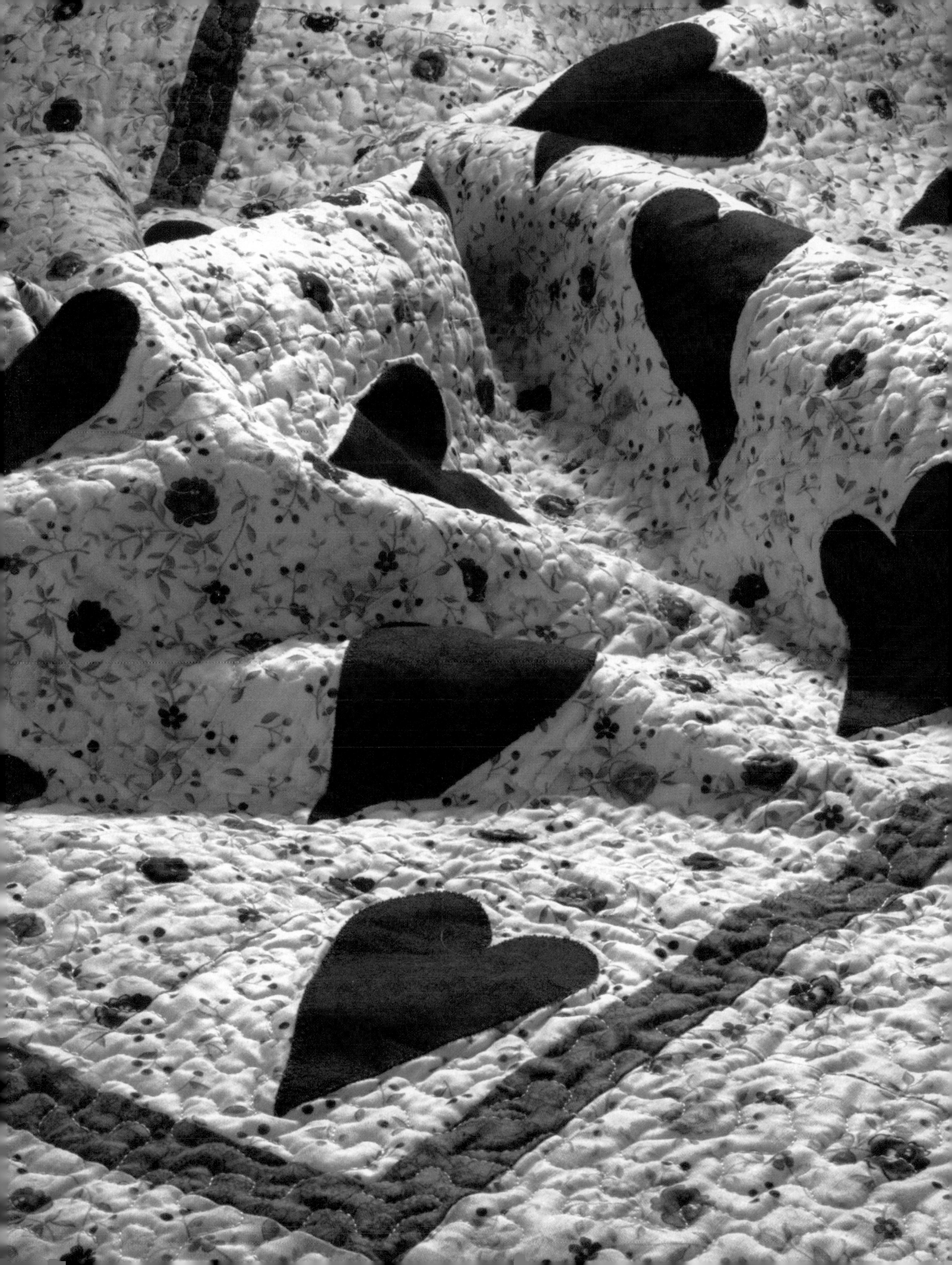

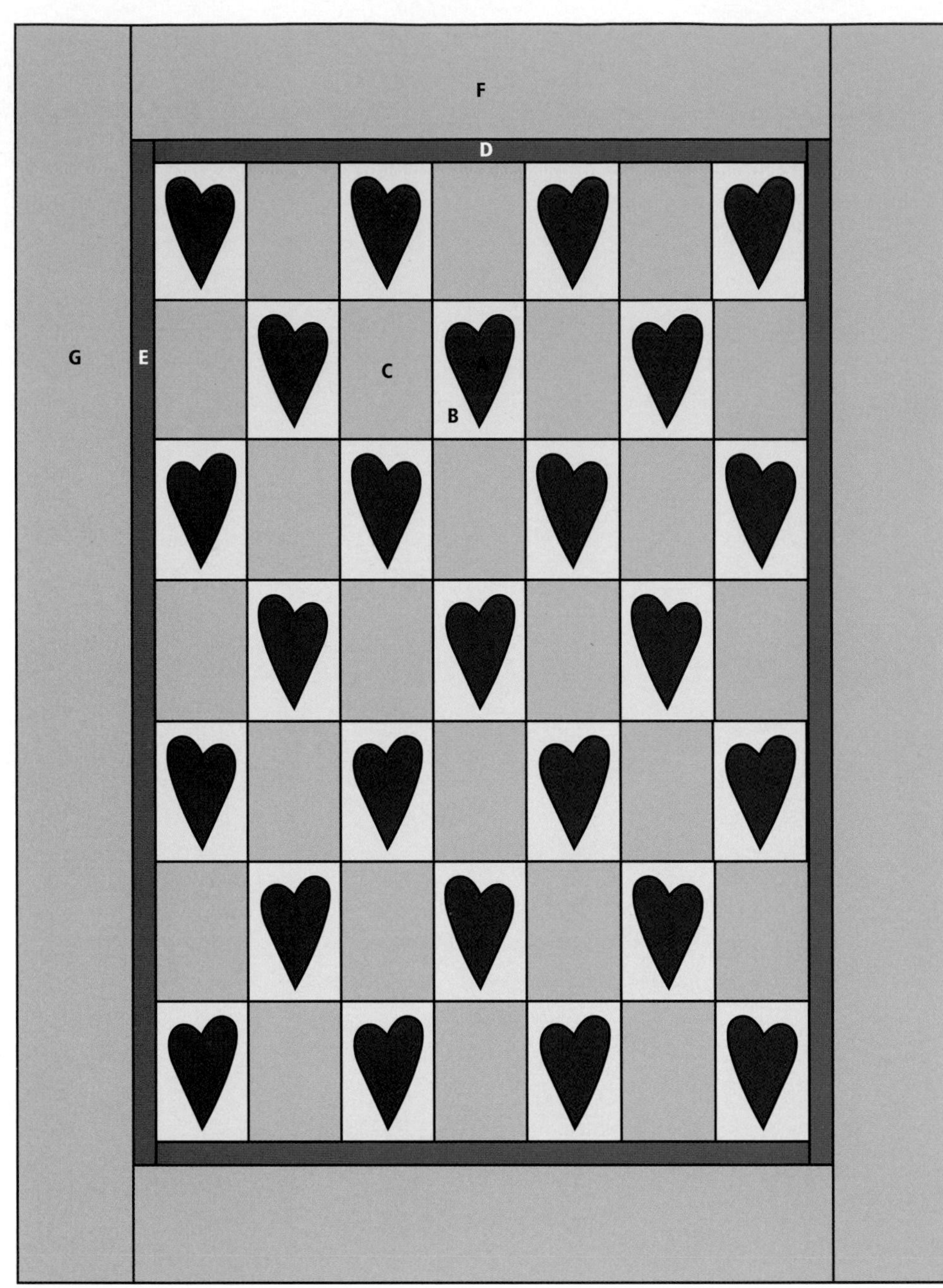

Hearts Quilt Layout

Fabric 1 - yellow floral

Fabric 2 – yellow print

Fabric 3 – red

Fabric 4 – blue

Construction

Sew ¼" seams with right sides together unless otherwise noted.

Heart Block

Finished size: 4" x 6"
(Fig. 1. Make 25 blocks.)

Fig 1

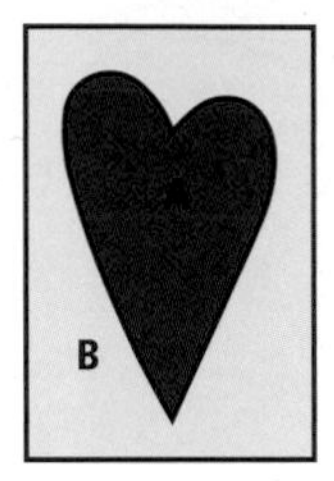

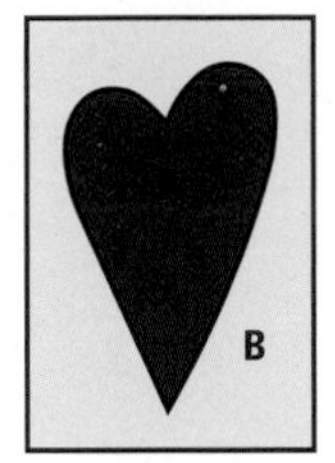

1. Center and then fuse one heart (A) over each small print rectangle (B).

2. Hand or machine appliqué around the hearts in thread that matches the heart fabric (see General Instructions, pages 134–135.)

Assembly

1. Sew together seven blocks in a row, beginning with a heart block and alternating with a floral print block (C) (Fig. 2). Repeat three times for a total of four rows. Press seams in one direction.

2. Sew together seven blocks in a row, beginning with a floral print block (C) and alternating with a heart block (Fig. 3). Repeat twice for a total of three rows. Press seams in opposite direction.

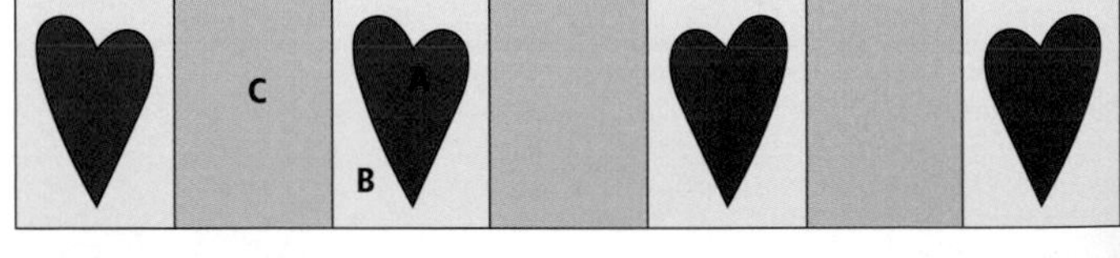

Fig. 2

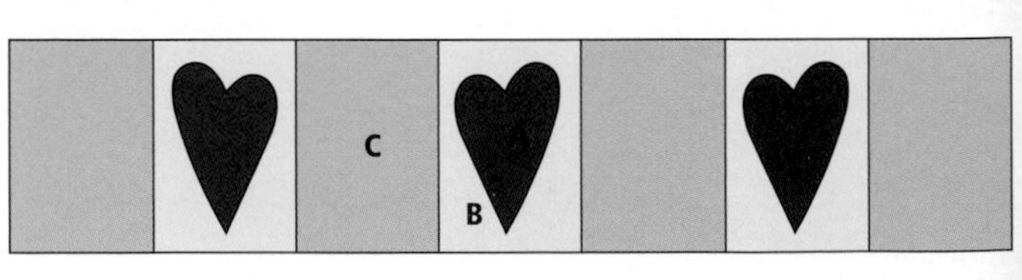

Fig. 3

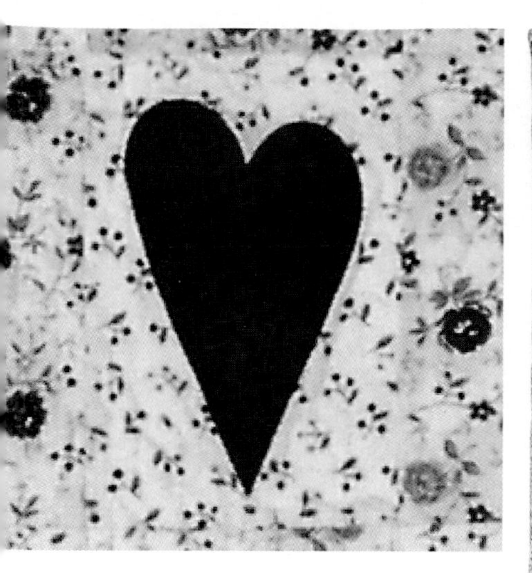

3. Sew together the seven rows, beginning with a heart block row and alternating with a floral print block row. Press seams in one direction.

4. Sew the top and bottom strips (D) of the inner border to the quilt; press and trim to fit. Piece three strips (E) together. Cut strip in half. Then sew the side strips (E) to the sides of the quilt; press and trim to fit.

5. Sew the floral strips (F) to the top and bottom of the quilt; press and trim to fit.

6. Piece together the remaining floral strips (G); press. Cut strips in half for the sides of the quilt. Sew the borders (G) to the sides of the quilt; press and trim to fit.

Quilting and Finishing

(See General Instructions pages 137–141)

1. Layer and baste together the quilt top, batting, and backing in preparation for quilting.

2. Hand or machine quilt. For this quilt, I used a meandering (stippling) stitch over the entire background.

3. Finish the quilt by cutting and piecing 2¼" strips of straight-grain binding fabric. Sew binding around quilt using folded mitered corners. ❖

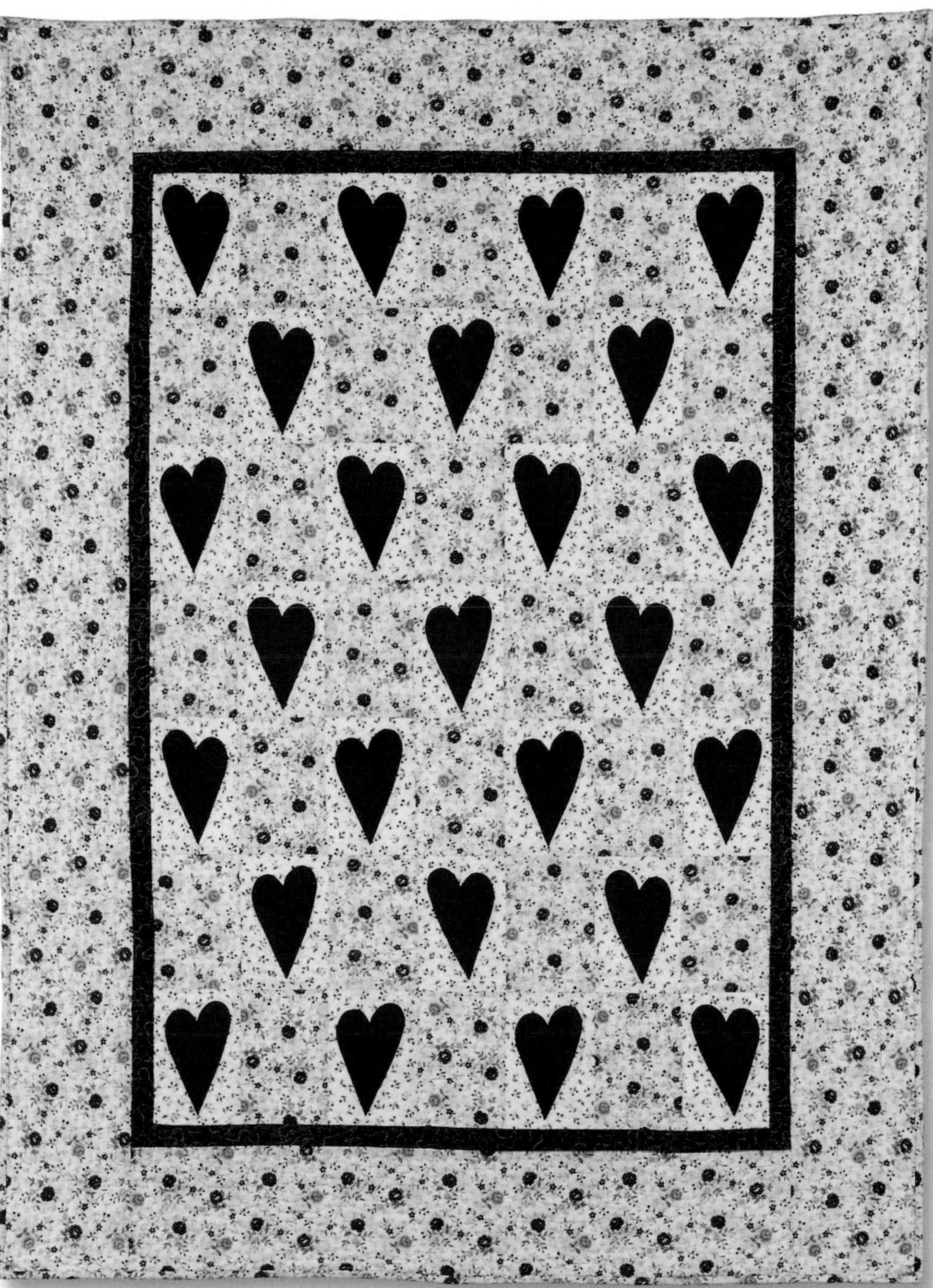

Hearts by Sandy Newman

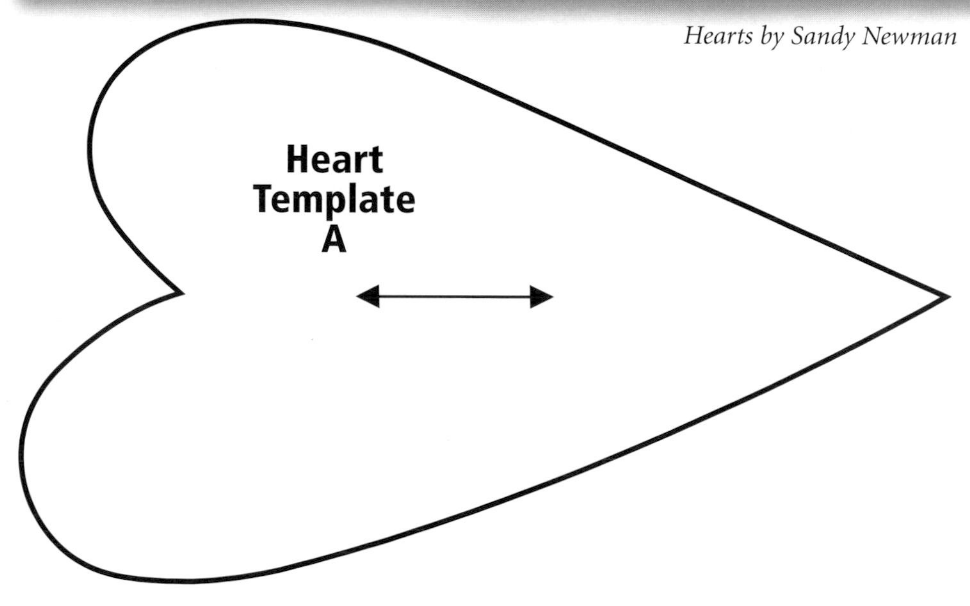

Gumballs

Designed and made by Sandy Newman; quilted by Ginger Hayes
Finished size: 50" x 60"

This quilt was designed as a gift for my nephew when he was born. It is a fun quilt to make because your fabrics can be as wild and bright as you want them to be, and they all look great with black and white. Choose tone-on-tone fabrics for your background rectangles and bright, highly patterned fabrics for your circles. (A tone-on-tone fabric—for example, a bright pink background with darker pink swirls—has two or three shades of the same color and adds texture.) Using this combination will give you a lot of contrast so that the gumballs stand out.

Materials

Yardage (based on 42" fabric, from selvage to selvage)

Fabric 1: ¼ yd. each of 13 assorted tones-on-tones
Fabric 2: ¼ yd. each of 13 assorted brights
Fabric 3*: 1¼ yds. black and white striped
Fabric 4: 1 yd. black and white print
Batting: 58" x 68"
½" bias maker
Basting glue

** This quilt uses the same fabric for the outside border and binding. If you use a different fabric for the binding, deduct ½ yd. from Fabric 1. The total yardage for binding should be ½ yd.*

Cutting

(See Quilt Layout Diagram)
Cut all fabrics crosswise, from selvage to selvage, unless otherwise instructed.

FABRIC 1

PIECE A: Cut two 8" x 10" rectangles from each tone-on-tone fabric for a total of 25 rectangles.

PIECE E: Cut eight 1½" squares from each tone-on-tone fabric for a total of 104* squares. ***NOTE:** Although these instructions yield 208 squares when Fabrics 1 and 2 are added together, the total number of squares needed for Piece E is actually 192.

FABRIC 2

PIECE B: Use the 5½" circle on page 88 to make a template for the gumballs (see General Instructions page 132). Use this template to draw two circles on the wrong side of each assorted bright fabric. Cut out fabric circles.

PIECE E: Cut eight 1½" squares from each bright fabric for a total of 104* squares.

FABRIC 3

BINDING: Cut six 2¼" strips.
PIECE C: Cut (25) 20" lengths of 1"-wide bias. Following bias maker's manufacturing instructions, fold each 20" length into ½"-wide folded bias strips.

FABRIC 4

BORDER F: Cut five 4½" strips.

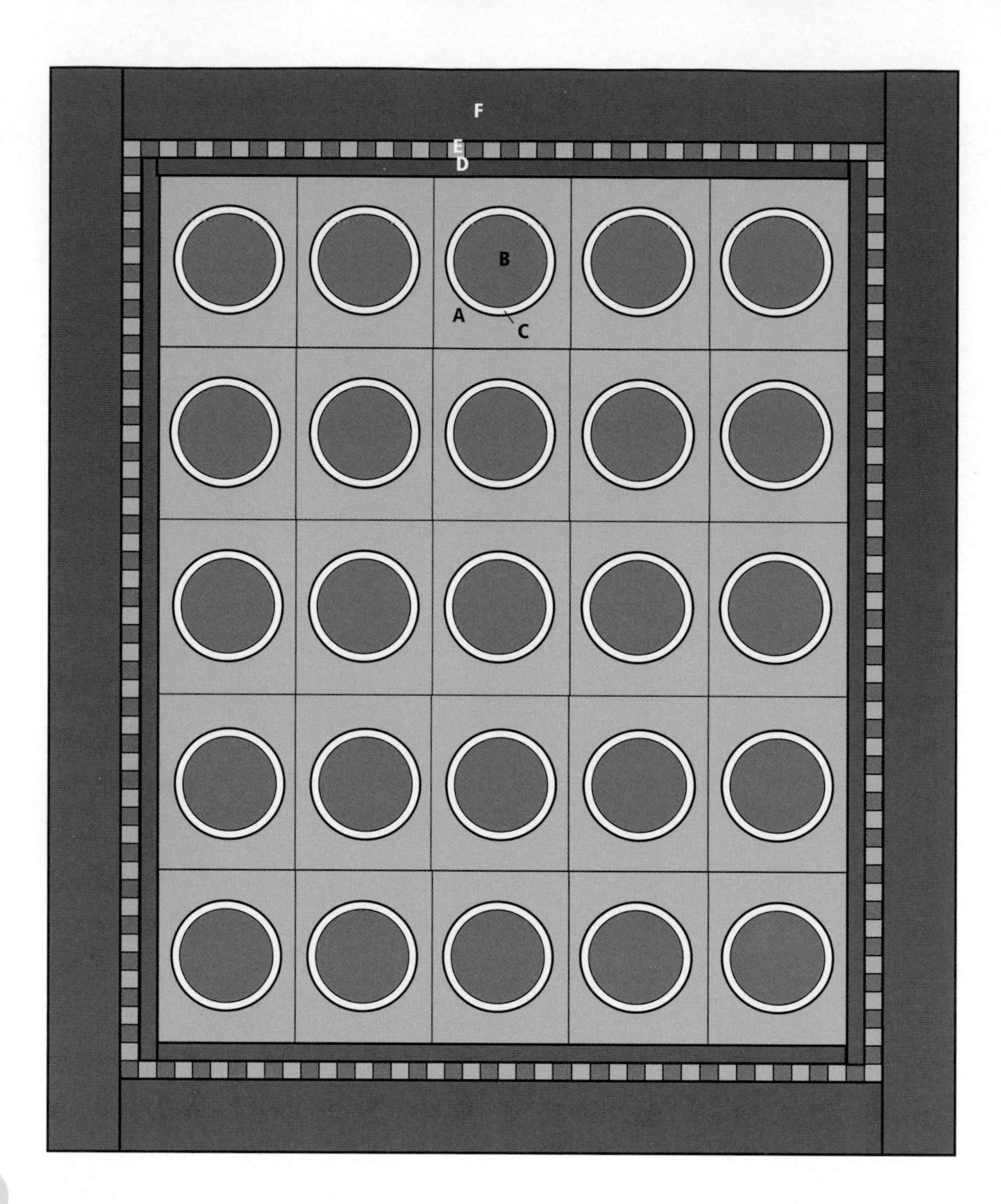

Gumballs Quilt Layout

Fabric 1 – assorted tone-on-tones

Fabric 2 – assorted brights

Fabric 3 – black-and-white striped

Fabric 4 – black-and-white print

Construction

Sew ¼" seams with right sides together unless otherwise noted.

Gumball Block

Finished size: 7½" x 9½"
(Fig. 1. Make 25 blocks.)

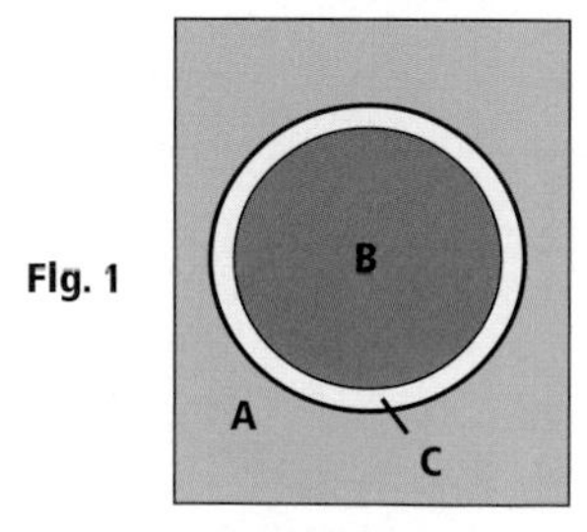

Flg. 1

To make each gumball block:

1. Center and pin a circle (B) to each background rectangle (A). Stitch a scant ¼" seam around the outside of the circle to hold it in place.

2. Use small dots of basting glue to attach bias strip around the outside of each circle. Be sure to cover your stitches. Appliqué the bias in place by stitching the inside and the outside of the bias to the circle and background (Fig. 2) (see General Instructions, Hand Appliqué, Steps 4 and 5, page 135).

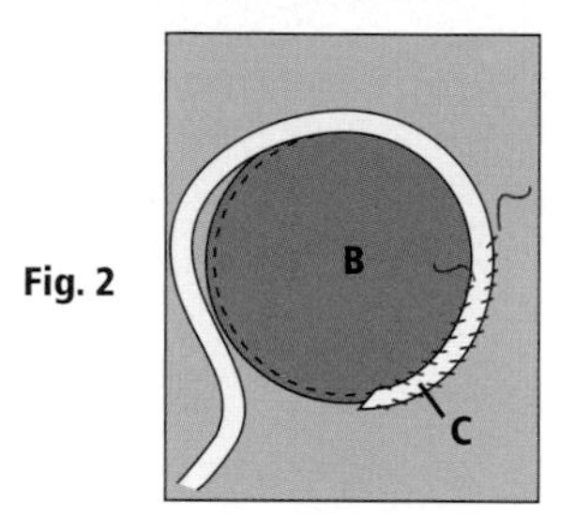

Fig. 2

3. To end the bias circle, fold back bias to where the stripes match and trim excess bias, if necessary, and complete stitching.

Assembly

1. Lay out the blocks in a pleasing arrangement, referring to quilt layout. Sew horizontal sets of five blocks together to form five rows. Press seams in one direction, then alternate direction for each row (Fig 3). Then sew the five rows together. Press seams in one direction. Your quilt should measure 38" x 48".

2. Lay out two sets of 40 squares (E) from the bright and tone-on-tone fabrics in an alternating arrangement of colors and fabrics. Sew squares together to get two 40-square rows each for top and bottom borders. The borders should measure 1½" x 40½" each.

3. Lay out two sets of 52 squares (E) from the bright and tone-on-tone fabrics in an alternating arrangement of colors and fabrics. Sew squares together to get two 52-square rows each to create side borders. Borders should measure 1½" x 52½".

4. If your quilt top and borders are the correct measurements, cut out five 1¾"strips from Fabric 4. If your measurements are

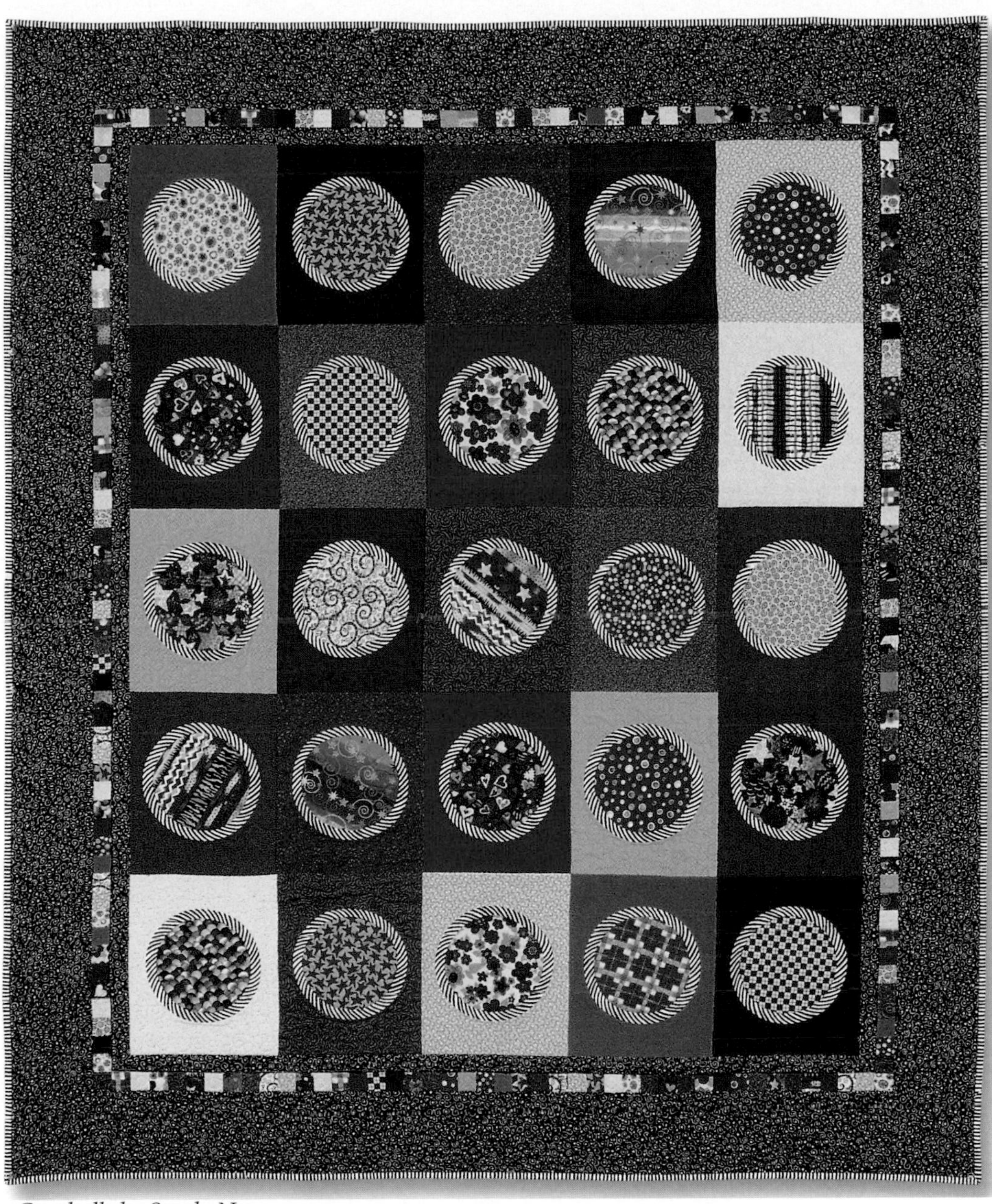

Gumballs by Sandy Newman

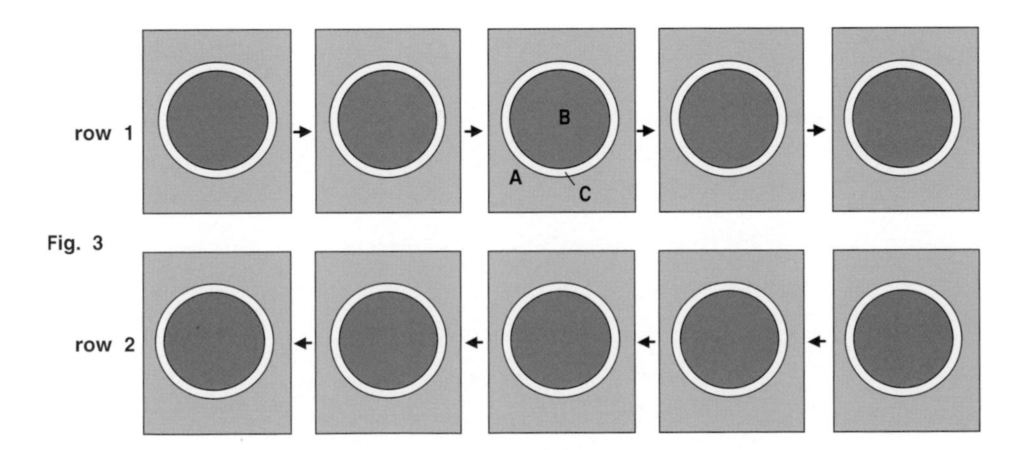

different, you will need to calculate a new width for inner Border D (see General Instructions, Adding Squared Borders, page 136).

5. Sew a strip D to top and bottom of quilt top; press and trim to fit.

6. Piece together three Border D strips. Cut border strip in half. Sew a strip to each side of quilt; press and trim to fit.

7. Sew top and bottom pieced borders to quilt top and bottom; press.

8. Sew side pieced borders to sides of quilt; press.

9. To create the outer border, sew two 4½" strips (F) to the top and bottom of the quilt; press and trim to fit.

10. Piece together the remaining outer border strips (F), cut in half, to create two 4½" strips.

11. Sew strips (F) to the sides of the quilt; press and trim to fit.

Quilting and Finishing

(See General Instructions pages 137–141)

1. Layer and baste together the quilt top, batting, and backing in preparation for quilting.

2. Hand or machine quilt. For each gumball I quilted a freeform shape that coordinated with the print fabric. I filled the rectangle backgrounds with a squiggle pattern. I used "stitch in the ditch" along the narrow borders and a squiggle line in the pieced border with a large curlicue design in the outer border.

3. Finish the quilt by piecing 2¼" strips of straight-grain binding fabric. Sew binding around quilt using folded mitered corners. ❖

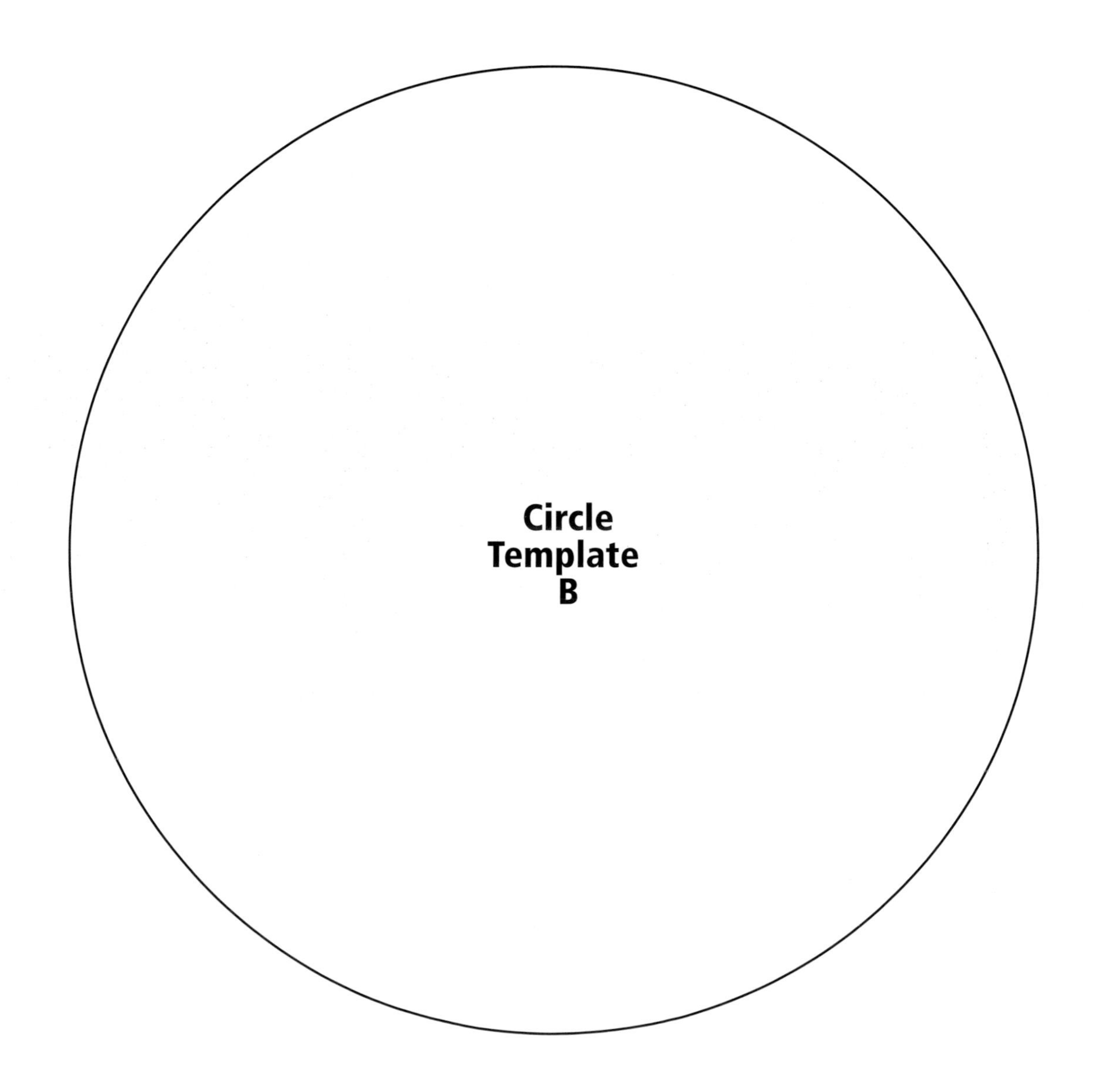

Laura Nownes

MY PASSION FOR MAKING QUILTS IS AN EXTENSION OF MY LOVE OF SEWING. I BEGAN hand sewing doll clothes at an early age. After completing the traditional first project in 4-H, an apron, I was asked to assist younger members in learning the basics. My first formal summer school teacher sent a note to my parents encouraging them to help me continue my desire for more. Against the wishes of my father, my mother rented a simple straight stitch sewing machine for me to use for three months. (My father thought this to be just another whim, like the accordion and ice skating lessons.) I purchased some fabric with my babysitting money and made a shirt for my father. He was so touched by the gift, it didn't matter that the shirt never fit properly. He took me to the sewing machine shop and paid off the balance on the machine.

After taking my first sampler quilt class in 1979, I knew I had found a lifelong interest. My connection with Diana McClun in 1980 allowed me to share my talents in the classroom at Diana's quilt shop, Empty Spools. My first love is teaching and although I teach a variety of classes, my primary focus has always been on the beginning quilter. I enjoy working with simple traditional patterns, updating, them with new fabrics and setting options. Diana and I have easily made over a hundred quilts and written five best selling books on quiltmaking, including *Quilts! Quilts!! Quilts!!!, Quilts Galore!, Quilts, Quilts and More Quilts!, Say It with Quilts, and Q is for Quilts.* We have worked together on television programs, with study groups and in seminars touching thousands of students, giving them a start in the basics of quiltmaking. We formed Teacher Development Seminars as a result of our commitment to the continuing education of quiltmaking. We also facilitate a teachers' retreat which is designed to train teachers in developing new classes.

Star Flowers

Designed and made by Laura Nownes; quilted by Kathy Sandbach
Finished size: 63" x 63"

The inspiration for this design evolved from a collection of Sawtooth Star blocks. I was working on a school quilt with a group of moms and wanted a design that included more than just the stars. The large Star Flower pattern was a result of playing with the blocks on a design wall in a variety of settings. The birdhouse block was an afterthought and added more interest to the borders. A variety of sky-like fabrics were used for the background. The Sawtooth Stars and birdhouse were created using a color combination of yellow, orange, red, and blue scraps that complemented each other as well as the background and checkerboard fabrics. Yardage requirements below indicate the amounts needed for one fabric. If a scrappy look is desired, break the amounts down according to the number of fabrics used.

Materials

Yardage (based on 42" fabric, from selvage to selvage)

- Fabric 1: 2¼ yds. assorted blues
- Fabric 2: 2 yds. assorted print scraps (stars)
- Fabric 3: ¼ yd. green
- Fabric 4: ⅛ yd. dark print
- Fabric 5: 1 yd. assorted print scraps (birdhouses)
- Fabric 6: ¾ yd. yellow check print
- Fabric 7: 1 yd. light print
- Backing: 3¾ yds.
- Batting: 3¾ yds.
- Binding: ½ yd.

Cutting

Cut all fabric crosswise, from selvage to selvage, unless otherwise instructed.

Sawtooth Star Blocks

(Fig. 1)

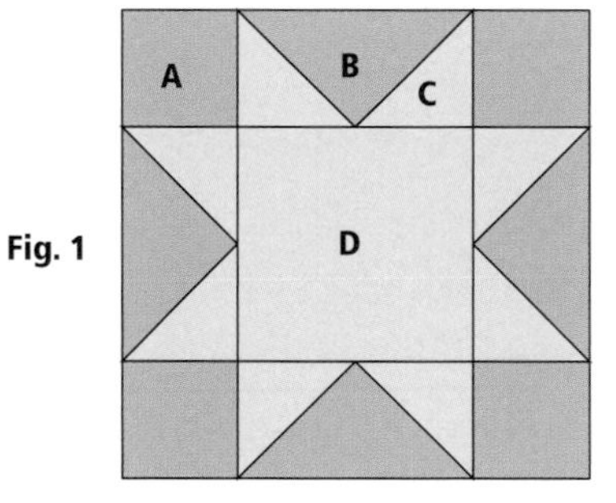

Fig. 1

FABRIC 1

Cut (24) 2" strips. Then, cut as follows:

Piece A: Cut nine of these strips into 2" squares (180 total).

Piece B: Cut 15 of these strips into 2" x 3½" pieces (180 total).

FABRIC 2

Piece C: Cut eight 2" squares per block (360 total).

Piece D: Cut one 3½" square per block (45 total).

Stems/flowerpot Blocks

(Fig. 2)

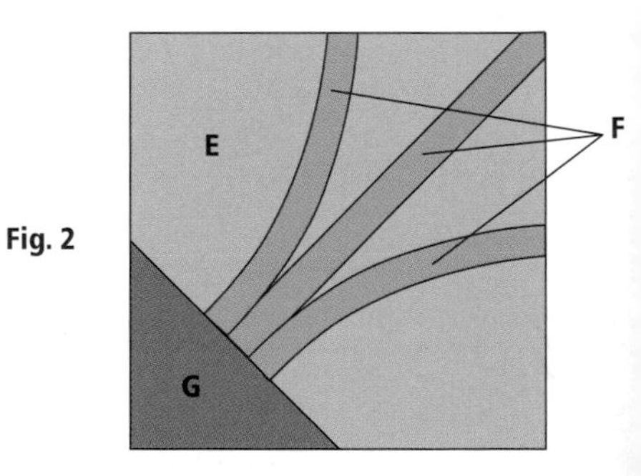

Fig. 2

FABRIC 1

Piece E: Cut two 6½" strips. Then cut these strips into 6½" squares (nine total).

FABRIC 3

Piece F: Cut (27) 1½" x 7" strips (cut on the bias).

FABRIC 4

Piece G: Cut one 3½"strip. Then cut this strip into 3½" squares (nine total).

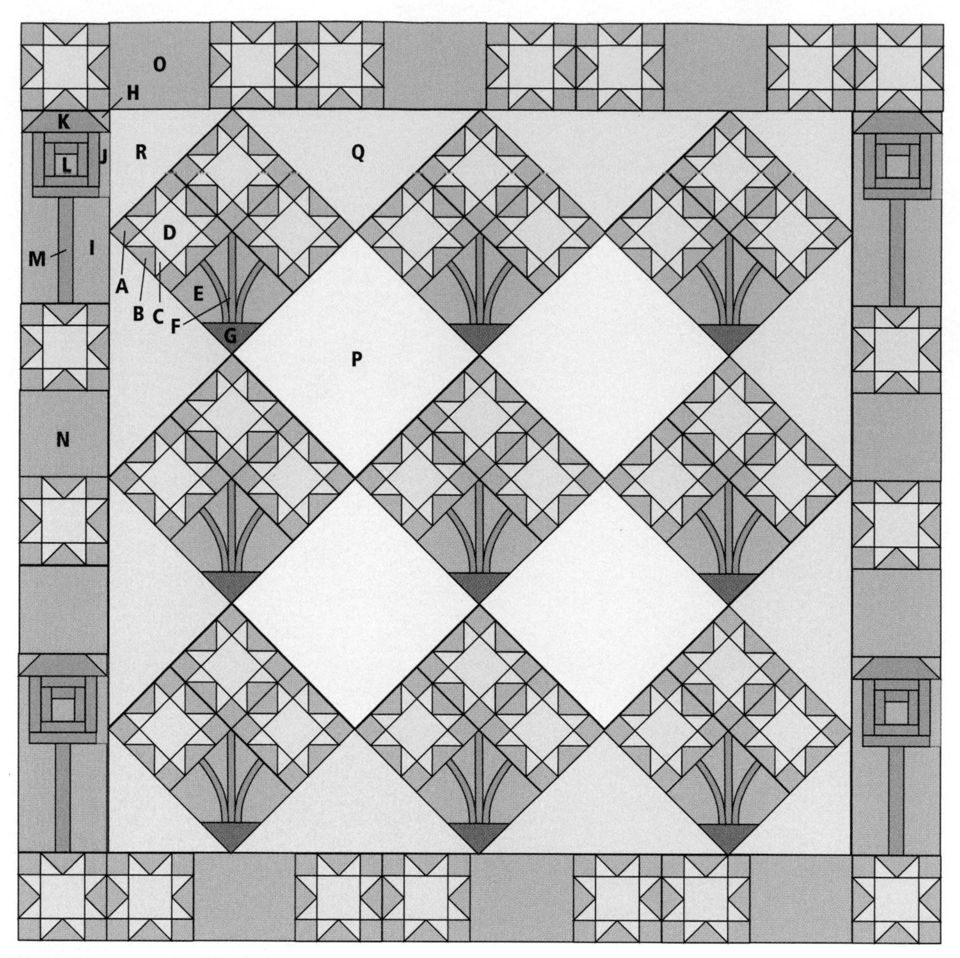

Star Flowers Quilt Layout

Fabric 1 - assorted blues

Fabric 2 - assorted print scraps (stars)

Fabric 3 - green

Fabric 4 - dark print

Fabric 5 - assorted print scraps (birdhouses)

Fabric 6 - yellow check print

Fabric 7 - light print

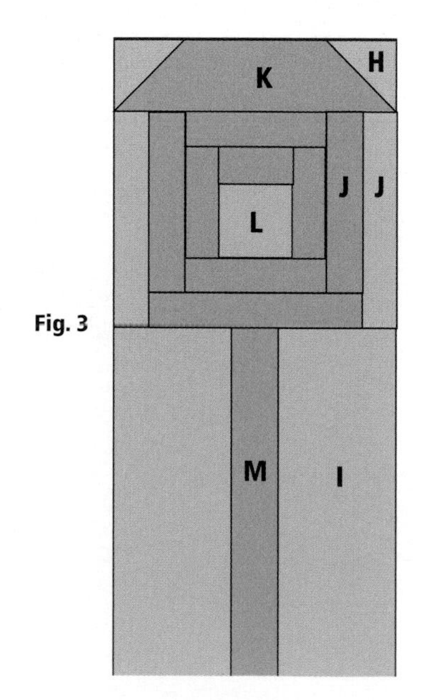

Fig. 3

Birdhouse Blocks

(Fig. 3)

FABRIC 1

PIECE H: Cut one 2" strip. Then cut this strip into 2" squares (eight total).

PIECE I: Cut two 3" strips.

PIECE J: Cut two 1¼" strips. Then cut these strips into 1¼" x 6½" pieces (eight total).

PIECE L: Cut one 2½" square per block (four total).

FABRIC 5

PIECE K: Cut one 2" x 6½" piece per block (four total).

HOUSE FRONTS: Cut 1¼" strips from a variety of fabrics. Sample quilt uses four strips per block (need 16 total).

PIECE M: Cut one 1½" strip.

Border Blocks

(See Quilt Layout Diagram)

FABRIC 1

PIECE N: Cut four 6½" squares.

PIECE O: Cut six 6½" x 7½" pieces.

Alternate Blocks

(See Quilt Layout Diagram)

FABRIC 6

PIECE P: Cut four 12½" squares.

Side and Corner Triangles

(See Quilt Layout Diagram)

FABRIC 7

PIECE Q: Cut two 18" squares. Cut the squares into quarters diagonally to make eight side triangles.

PIECE R: Cut two 10½" squares. Cut the squares in half diagonally to make four corner triangles.

Construction

Sew ¼" seams with right sides together unless otherwise noted.

Sawtooth Star

Finished size: 6"

(See Fig. 1. Make 45 blocks.)

To make each Sawtooth Star block:

1. Place a background piece (B) and a star point square (C) right sides together (Fig. 4).

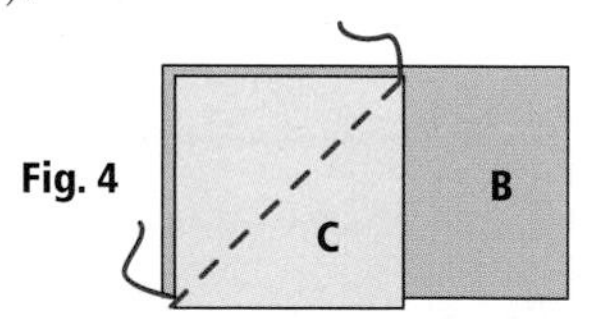

Fig. 4

2. Stitch diagonally across the square, through both fabrics.

3. Trim seams ¼" beyond the stitching line (Fig. 5), and press the resulting star point back over the stitching line.

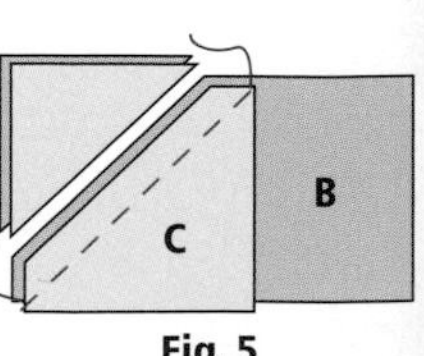

Fig. 5

Star Flowers by Laura Nownes

4. Place another square (C) onto the background piece (B), and repeat Steps 2–3 (Fig. 6).

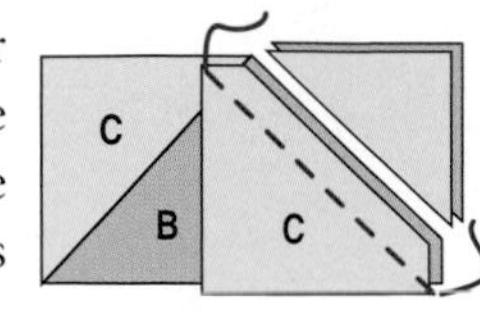

Fig. 6

5. Repeat Steps 1–4 three times (need four star point units total per block).

6. Lay out all the pieces for each star (Fig. 7). Sew the pieces together in rows to form the finished block; press the seams in the direction of the arrows.

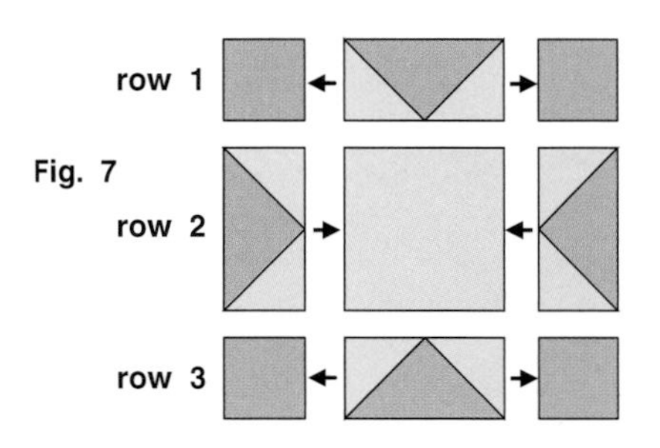

Fig. 7

7. Sew Rows 1–3 together; press in one direction. Alternate pressing for each subsequent block.

Stems/flowerpot

Finished size: 6" x 6"
(See Fig. 2. Make nine blocks.)

To make each stems/flowerpot block:

1. Press a diagonal crease in a background square (E).

2. Press the stem pieces in half lengthwise, wrong sides together.

3. Position one stem onto the right side of the background square with the raw edges even with the diagonal crease and the bottom of the stem 1½" above the bottom corner. Then stitch the stem ¼" from its raw edge (Fig. 8).

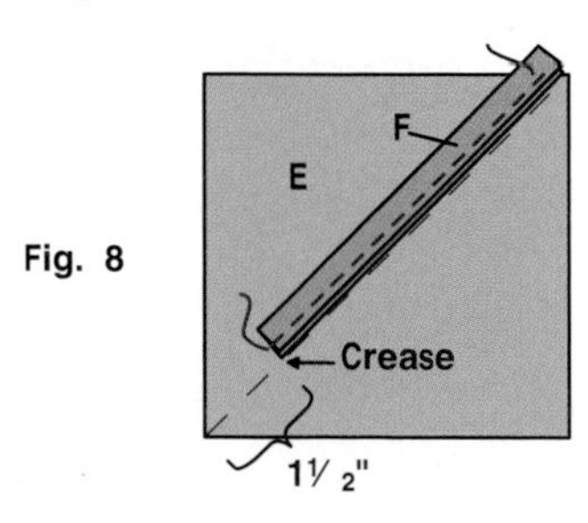

Fig. 8

4. Press the folded edge of the stem over the stitching line and sew in place to the background square, either by hand or machine.

5. Measure 2¾" down from the top point on each side of the background square and mark where to place the top of the side stems. Align the bottom of the stems with the center stem and ease the strips into symmetrical curves. Sew the side stems using the same pressing and stitching technique as for the center stem (Fig. 9).

6. Place a square of flowerpot fabric (G) onto the bottom corner of the block. Stitch across the square diagonally. Then cut ¼" beyond the stitching line (Fig. 10).

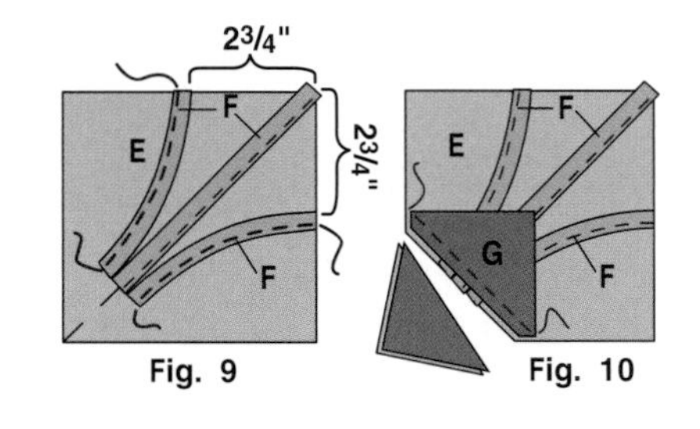

Fig. 9 Fig. 10

7. Press the resulting triangle of flowerpot fabric over the stitching line to complete the block.

Star Flower

Finished size: 12" x 12"
(See Fig. 11. Make nine blocks.)

To make each Star Flower block:

1. Sew together two Sawtooth Star blocks. Press seams in one direction.

2. Sew together one stem/flowerpot block and one Sawtooth Star block (Fig. 11). Press seams in the opposite direction.

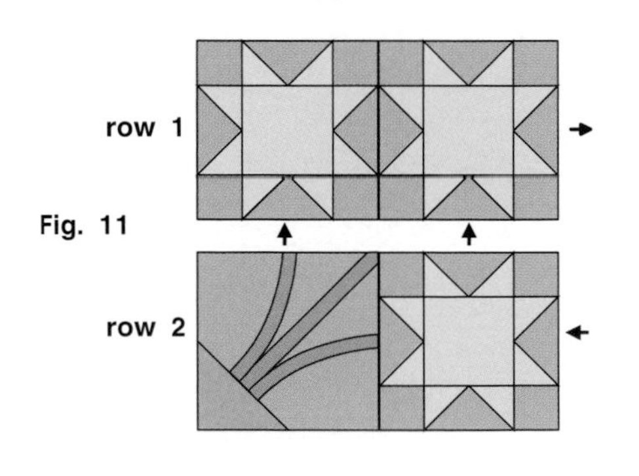

Fig. 11

3. Sew Rows 1 and 2 together; press.

Birdhouse

Finished size: 6" x 13½"
(See Fig. 3. Make 4 blocks.)

To make each birdhouse block:

1. Sky/roof unit: Place two background squares (H) onto a roof (K) piece. Stitch across the squares diagonally (as for Sawtooth Stars, and then cut 1/4" beyond the stitching line (Fig. 12). Press seams away from the center.

Fig. 12

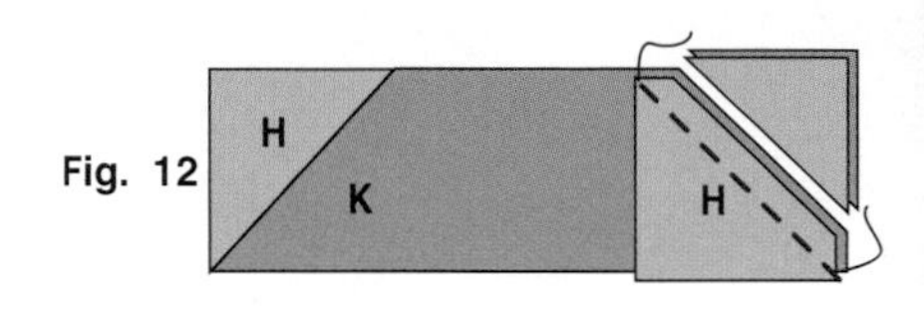

2. House unit: With right sides together, stitch a center (L) square to a 1½" strip of house fabric (Fig. 13). Trim the strip even with the edges of the square. Press seams away from the center (Fig. 14).

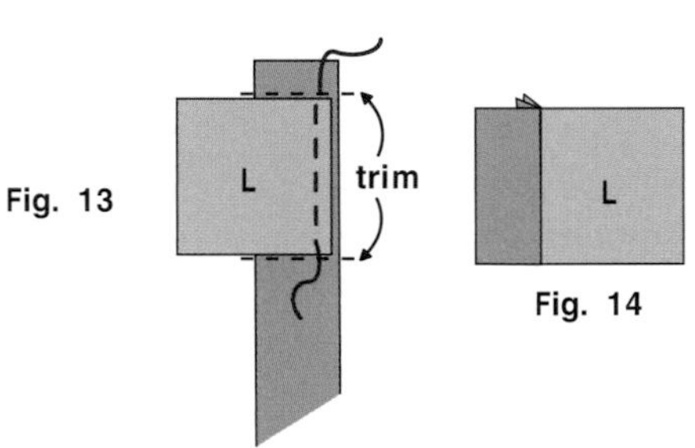

Fig. 13 Fig. 14

3. With right sides together, stitch the unit to another strip of the fabric (Fig. 15). Press the strip away from the center square and trim it even with the edges of the first unit.

4. Continue adding strips in this manner around the center square, using each fabric in two positions and a total of four fabrics per block (Fig. 16).

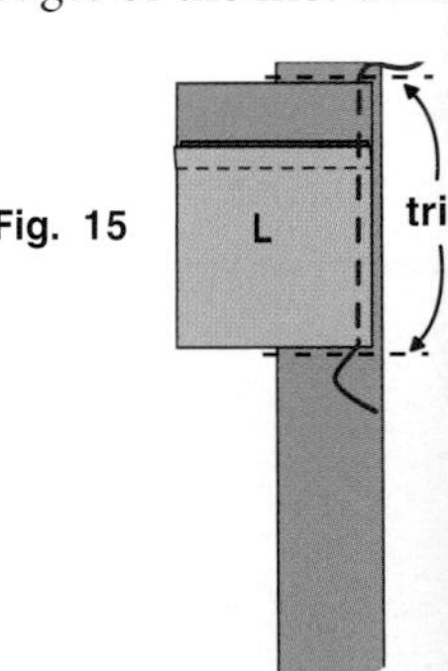

Fig. 15

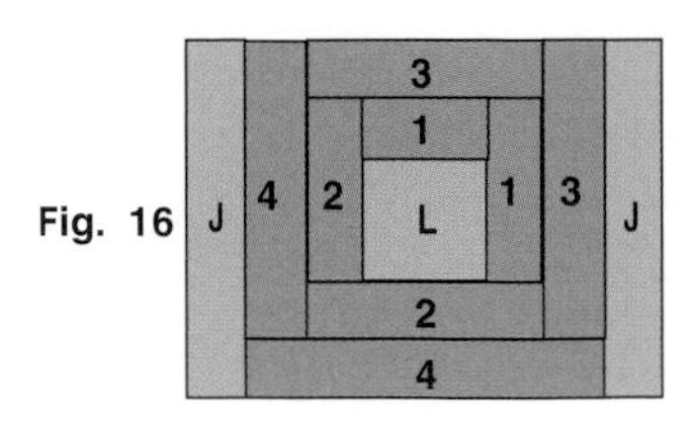

Fig. 16

5. Sew background pieces (J), right sides together, to the sides of the birdhouse. Press toward J (Fig. 16).

6. Background/pole unit: Sew together the background (I) strips and the pole (M) strip. Then cut the set of strips apart every 8" (Fig. 17).

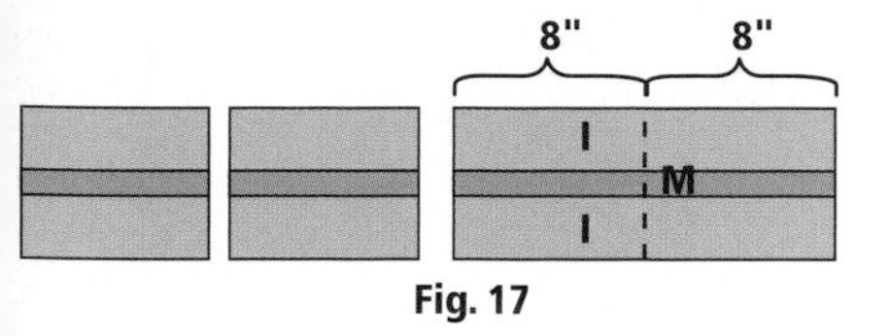

Fig. 17

7. Sew together all the units (Fig. 3) to complete the birdhouse block; press.

Assembly

1. Lay out all the Star Flower blocks, alternate blocks (P), and side (Q) and corner (R) triangles. A design wall is helpful for this step. **Note:** If necessary, trim the alternate blocks to match the finished size of your Star Flower blocks.

2. Sew together all the pieces in diagonal rows (Fig. 18). **Note:** The side and corner triangles are larger than needed to allow for straightening the edges and cutting to the exact length needed for the pieced borders.

3. Sew together the required number of Sawtooth Star blocks, border blocks (N), and birdhouse blocks for the side borders (Fig. 18).

4. Sew together the required number of Sawtooth Star blocks and border blocks (O) for the top and bottom borders (Fig. 18).

5. Measure the lengths of the borders to determine how much fabric to trim from the side and corner triangles to allow for the center quilt borders to fit properly. Place a large ruler at the corners when cutting to assure an accurate right angle.

6. Attach the sides and then the top and bottom pieced borders to complete the quilt top.

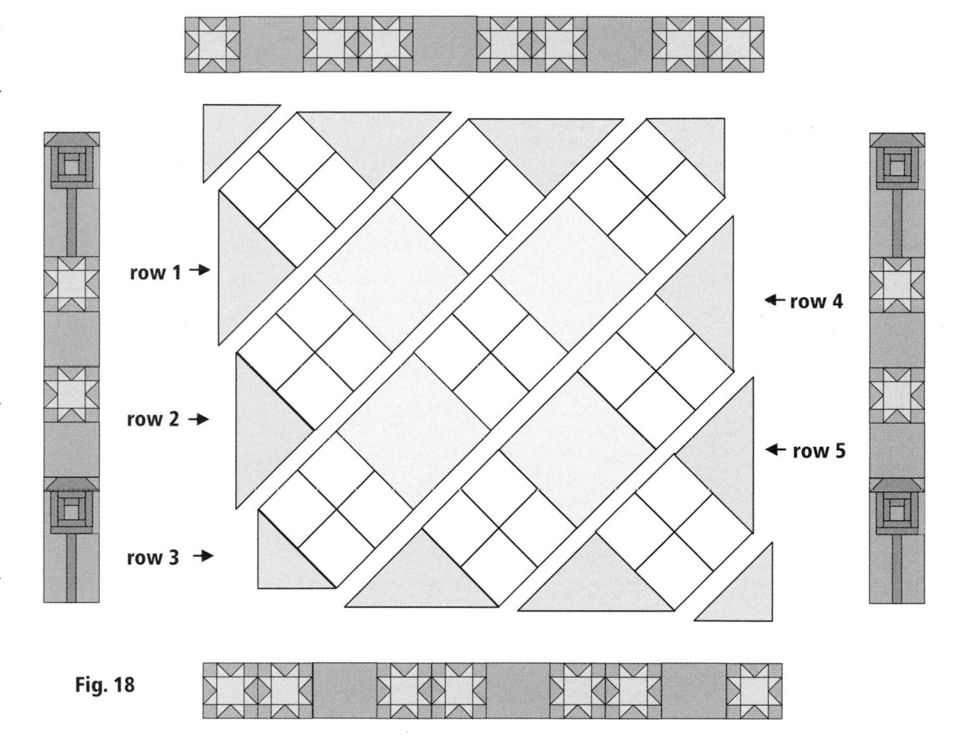

Fig. 18

Quilting and Finishing

(See General Instructions pages 137–141)

1. Layer and baste the quilt top, batting, and backing in preparation for quilting.

2. Hand or machine quilt. The sample quilt has many "garden critters" (snails, birds, frogs, rabbits, and so on) in the large spaces (see close-up photo on front cover). Coloring books and cookie cutters are a good source of inspiration for these types of designs. The center star flower motif is stitched in the ditch.

3. Finish the quilt with 1⅞" folded mitered corner binding.

4. Finish the quilt by cutting and piecing 2¼" strips of straight-grain binding fabric. Sew binding around quilt using folded mitered corners.❖

Bethlehem Star

Designed and made by Laura Nownes and Diana McClun; quilted by Kathy Sandbach
Large Star pattern from Quilts! Quilts!! Quilts!!!
Benicia Rose pattern designed by Adele Ingraham
Finished size: 55" x 55"

This quilt was designed for students who had completed both my beginning and intermediate level classes. It provides a piecing challenge while covering the following techniques: Y-seam construction (large star and Le Moyne Star), appliqué (Benicia Rose), and curved piecing (Drunkard's Path). Don't rush through this one. Accuracy is important every step of the way. The results are well worth the time invested.

Materials

Yardage (based on 42" fabric, from selvage to selvage)

Fabric 1: 2 yds. white
Fabric 2: 1¼ yds. blue
Fabric 3: ¼ yd. olive green
Fabric 4: ⅜ yd. floral
Fabric 5: ½ yd. red
Fabric 6: ⅝ yd. light gold
Fabric 7: ⅝ yd. blue green
Fabric 8: ⅛ yd. light blue
Fabric 9: ¾ yd. assorted red prints
Fabric 10: ⅛ yd. yellow
Fabric 11: 1 yd. assorted green prints
Backing: 3⅜ yds.
Binding: ⅜ yd.
Batting: 72" x 90"
Ruler with a 45-degree angle marking
Spray starch (optional)
10" square of plastic for templates

Cutting

(See Quilt Layout Diagram)
Cut all fabric crosswise, from selvage to selvage, unless otherwise instructed.

Large Center Star

Piece A: Cut the following fabrics into 2" strips as indicated.
Fabric 2: two 2" strips
Fabric 3: three 2" strips
Fabric 4: five 2" strips
Fabric 5: seven 2" strips
Fabric 6: four 2" strips

FABRIC 1

Piece E: Cut one 15½" square. Then cut the square twice on the diagonal to make four side triangles.

FABRIC 2

Piece G: Use Template G to cut four tips for the side triangles.

Bethlehem Star Quilt Layout

Le Moyne Star Block

(See Fig. 1. Make 4.)

Fig. 1

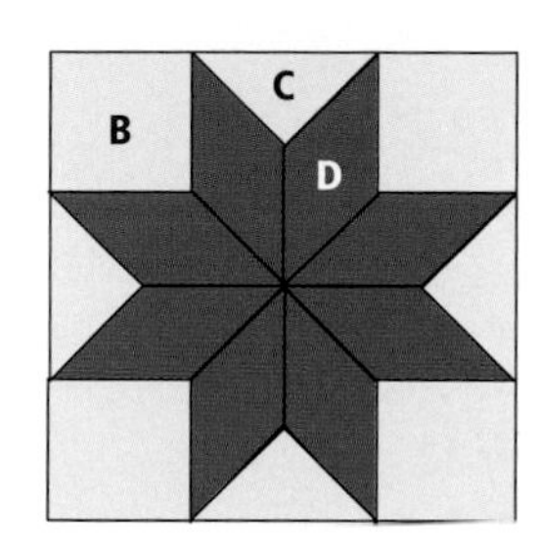

FABRIC 1

PIECE B: Cut two 4¼" strips. Then cut each strip into 4¼" squares for a total of 16 squares.

PIECE C: Cut one 7" strip. Cut this strip into four 7" squares. Then cut each square twice on the diagonal to make 16 triangles.

PIECE D: Cut four 2⅝" strips. Use the 45-degree angle on the ruler to cut 2⅝" diamonds (Fig. 2).

ig. 2

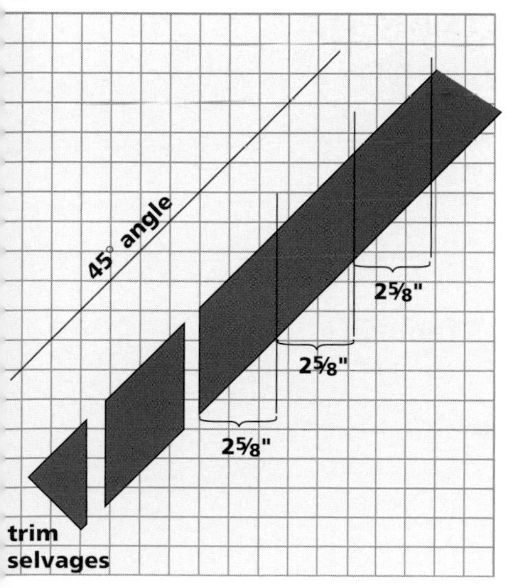

Drunkard's Path Border Block

(See Fig. 3. Make 92.)

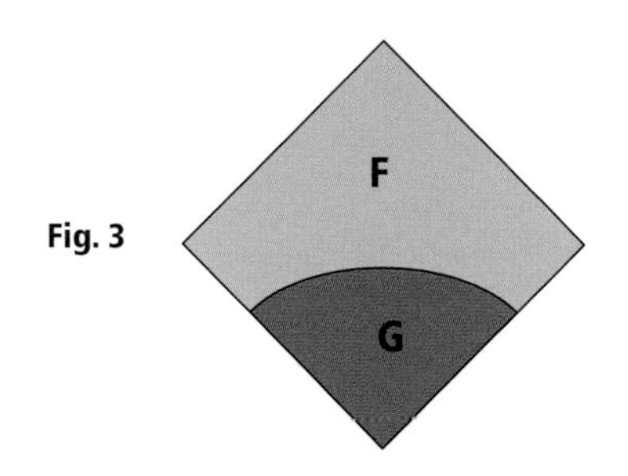

FABRIC 11

PIECE F: Cut eight 3½" strips. Cut each strip into 3½" squares for a total of 92 squares. Use Pattern F to make a plastic template. Use the template to mark the curve onto the wrong side of each square. Then cut on the marked line. Use a small pair of scissors to make three ⅛" clips into the curve, as indicated on Pattern F.

FABRIC 9

PIECE G: Cut six 2½" strips. Cut each strip into 2½" squares for a total of 92 squares. Use Pattern G to make a plastic template. Use the template to mark the curve onto the wrong side of each square. Then cut on the marked line. Use a small pair of scissors to make three ⅛" clips into the curve, as indicated on Pattern G.

Setting Triangles

FABRIC 6

PIECE H: Cut two 6½" strips. Cut each strip into 6½" squares for a total of 10 squares. Then, cut each square twice on the diagonal to create 40 triangles.

FABRIC 2

PIECE I: Cut three 6½" strips. Cut each strip into 6½" squares for a total of 13 squares. Then, cut each square twice on the diagonal to create 52 triangles.

Appliqué Border

FABRIC 7

PIECE K: Cut eight 1½" pieces on the bias.

PIECE N: Use Template N to cut 31 leaves. (If you prefer, you can also use scraps from other fabrics to create leaves.)

FABRIC 8

PIECE L: Use Template L to cut four flowers.

FABRIC 9

PIECE L: Use Template L to cut 12 flowers.

PIECE O: Use Template M to cut 55 berries.

FABRIC 10

PIECE M: Use Template M to cut 16 flower centers.

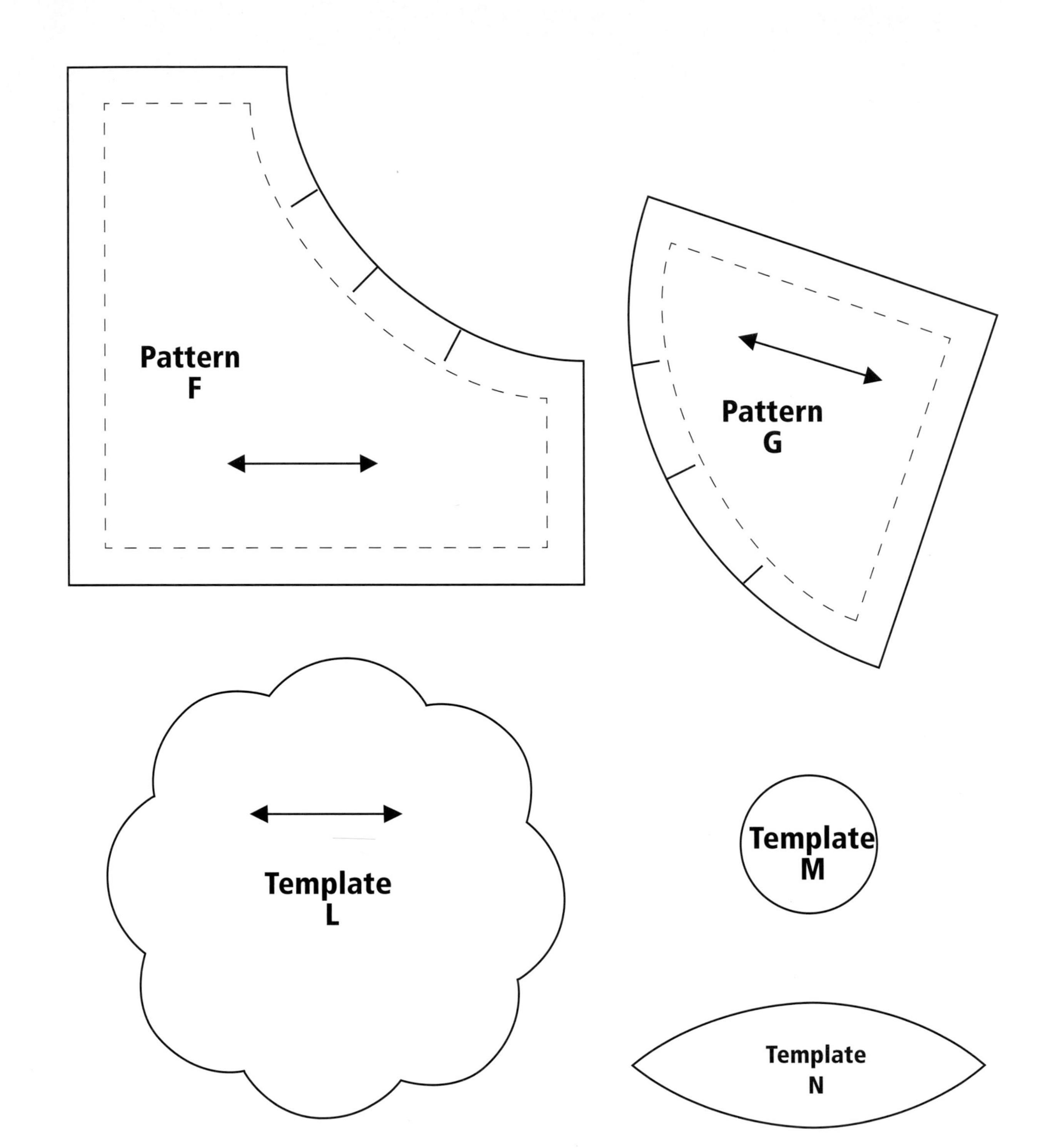
Pattern
F
Pattern
G
Template
L
Template
M
Template
N

Construction

Sew ¼" seams with right sides together unless otherwise noted.

Center Star

Finished size: 35"x 35"
(See Quilt Layout. Make 1 star.)

To make the center star:

1. Sew the 2" strips (A) into sets. Refer to the following table for the sewing sequence of the fabrics and the required number of sets. **NOTE:** A 1½" step is added with each strip (Fig. 4).

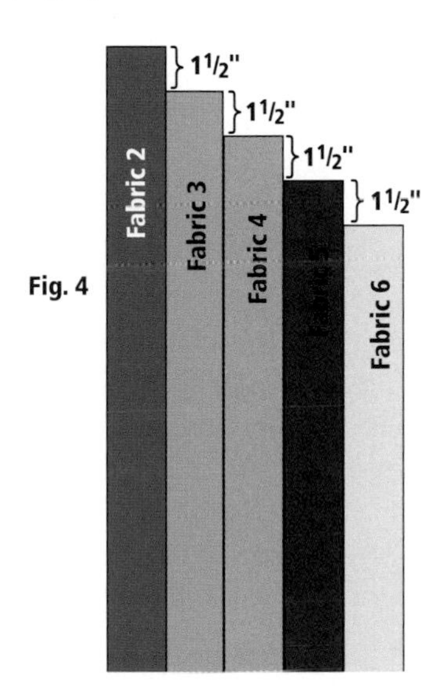

Fig. 4

	Fabric Sequence	Number of Sets*
Set 1	2-3-4-5-6	1½
Set 2	3-4-5-6-5	1½
Set 3	4-5-6-5-4	1

**Use 2" x 22" strips for the half-sets.*

2. Carefully press the seam allowances in the direction of the first strip in each set. Spray sizing is helpful to stabilize the sets in preparation for cutting.

3. Place Set 1 onto the cutting mat, positioning the 45-degree angle of the ruler even with the left-hand edge of the set. Remove the selvages and make a straight cut (Fig. 5). Maintaining the 45-degree angle, cut (16) 2" strips. Repeat this step for Sets 2 and 3, except cut only eight 2" strips from Set 3.

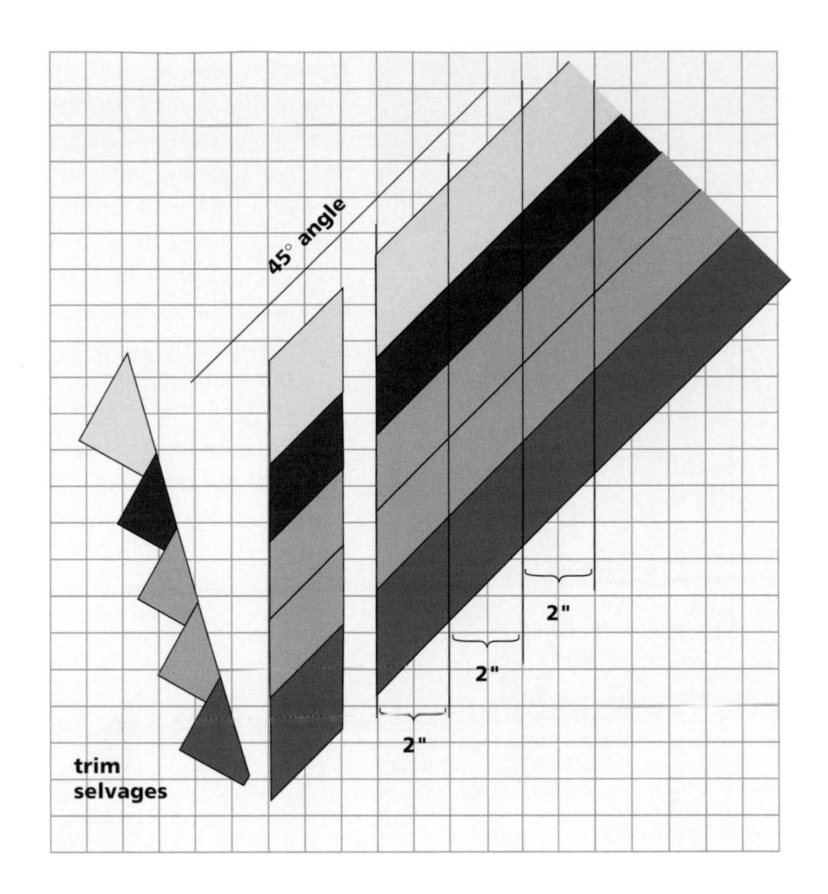

Fig. 5

4. Lay out the cut units as shown (Fig. 6). Then sew together to make a pieced diamond. Repeat to create a total of eight pieced diamonds.

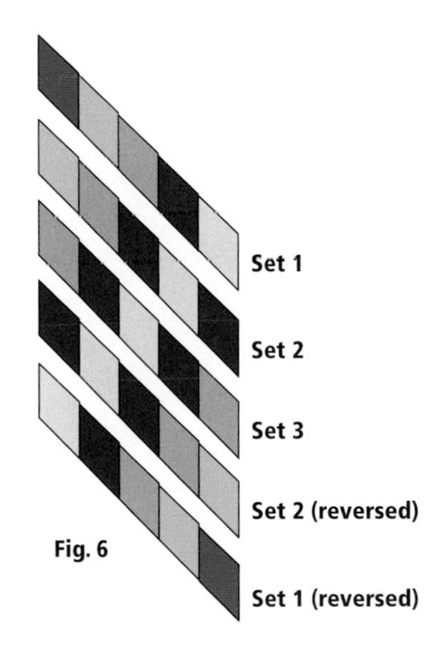

Fig. 6

TIP: Because the seams cross in opposite directions, place pins on both sides of the seam allowances at the intersections to prevent slipping while sewing.

5. Press all seams in one direction. Set diamond units aside until the Le Moyne Stars are finished.

Le Moyne Star

Finished size: 10¼" x 10¼"
(Fig. 1. Make 4 blocks.)

To make each Le Moyne Star:

6. The Le Moyne Stars are sewn together using Y-seams. Before constructing the blocks, lightly mark the ¼" seam allowance onto the wrong side of the pieces to indicate starting and stopping points of the stitching lines, as indicated by the dots (Fig. 7).

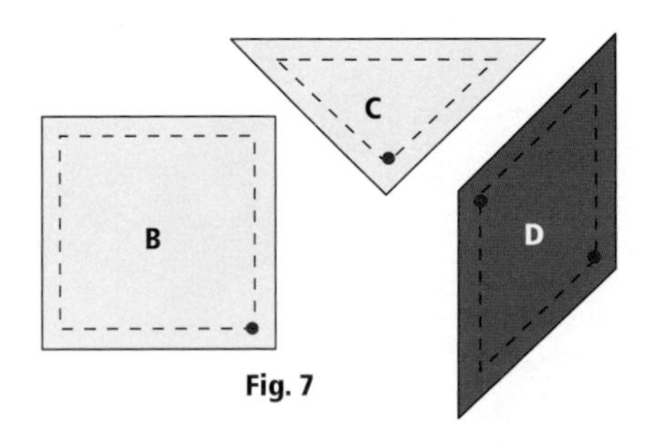

Fig. 7

Note: The cutting instructions for the Le Moyne Star block's background pieces (B and C) allow for possible variations in the finished size of your large center star. Depending on your fabrics and how accurately you have cut, sewn, and pressed the pieces in the large center star, you may need to trim the background pieces (B and C) to fit exactly into the corners of the large center star.

7. Right sides together, sew two diamonds (D) to the short sides of a background triangle (C); stop at the dots. Then, sew together the diamonds (Fig. 8). Press open the seams joining the diamonds.

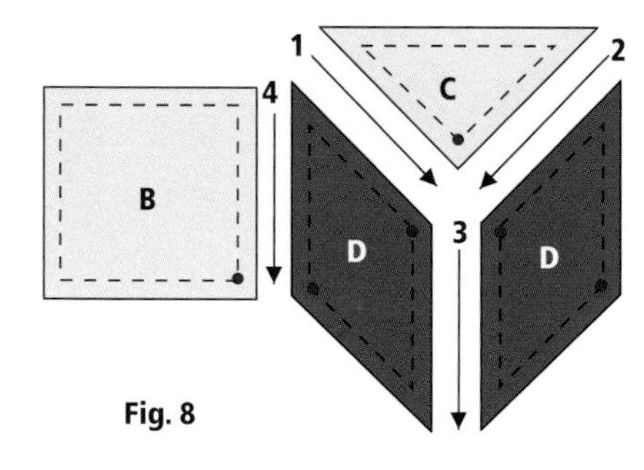

Fig. 8

8. Sew a corner square (B) to each pair of diamonds.

9. Sew two units together to make one half of the star (Fig. 9). Do not stitch beyond the dots.

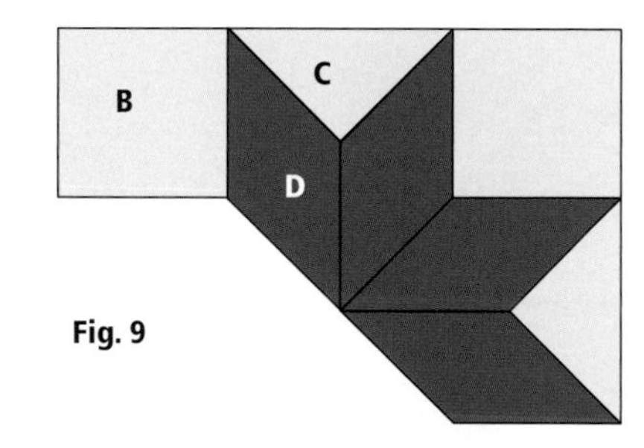

Fig. 9

10. Repeat Steps 6–8 to make the second half of the star. Sew the two halves together to complete the block. Press open the last seam, through the center of the star.

Center Star Completion

To complete the center star:

11. Press under curved edge of blue triangle tip (G). Sew wrong side of (G) to right side of side triangle (E) on ¼" seam line, matching raw edges (Fig. 10). Blind stitch curved edge into place on (E). Repeat for each side triangle (E).

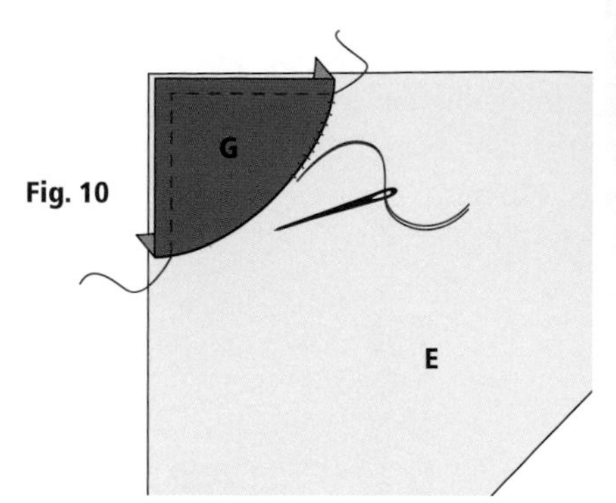

Fig. 10

12. Use Steps 1–4 for the Le Moyne Star block to complete the center star, except replace Piece C with Piece G/E, Piece D with a pieced diamond, and Piece B with a completed Le Moyne Star.

Drunkard's Path Border

To make the Drunkard's Path border:

13. Pin together Pieces F and G, right sides together, aligning the seam lines and easement clips, easing around the curve. Sew over pins, keeping an accurate ¼" seam allowance. Clip curves and press. Repeat this step to create a total of 92 units (Fig. 11).

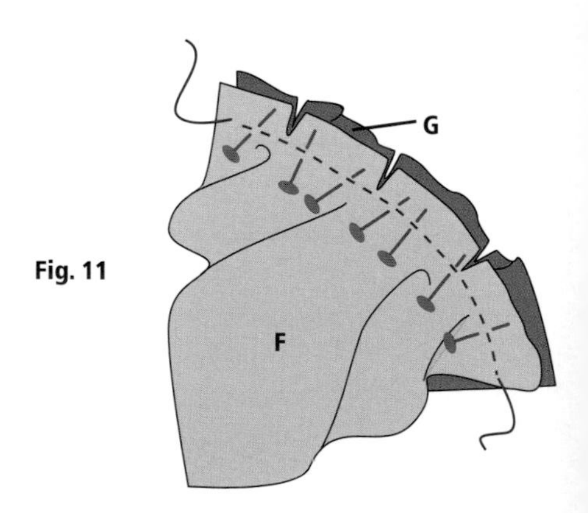

Fig. 11

14. Sew together the F/G units in diagonal rows with the inner (H) and outer (I) setting triangles (Fig. 12), being sure to join together the F/G units on the G side. Create a total of 28 units.

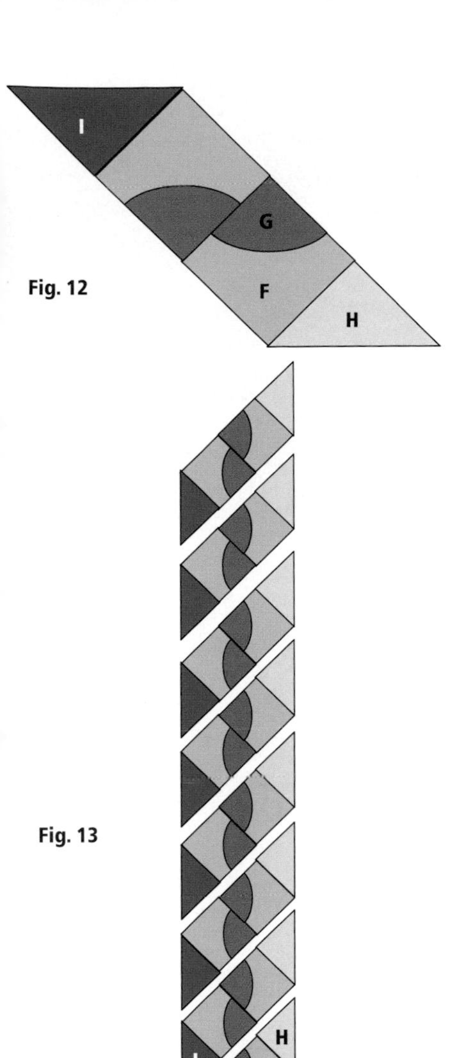

Adjustment Instructions

❖

1. Measure the four sides of the Drunkard's Path border to determine the average length of one side. Write this measurement on a piece of paper.
2. Measure the four sides of the large center star block to determine the average length of one side. Subtract this measurement from the measurement in Step 1. Then divide the difference by two. Finally, add ½" to this amount. This equals the cutting width of strip J.

15. For each side of the border, sew ten units into a row as shown. Then add three partial units (Fig. 13) and sew these to the end of the row. Straighten the edges.

Assembly

(Fig. 14)

At this point, the large center star block should measure 35" x 35". If it does not, you will need to adjust the following cutting instructions for the width of Border J. See the Adjustment Instructions (below) for help.

1. If quilt measurements are correct cut five 4" strips (J); if not, cut five determined-width strips (J).

2. Sew a strip (J) to each side of the quilt; press and trim to fit.

3. Piece remaining strips (J) together, press and cut strip in half. Sew cut strips (J) to top and bottom of quilt; press and trim to fit.

4. Center and sew four Drunkard's Path borders to the quilt sides, leaving extending seam allowance at both ends of quilt.

5. Attach the four corner units.

6. To create the vine (K), press a length of bias cut fabric in half lengthwise with the right side facing out. Pin the vine onto the fabric in the desired arrangement. **NOTE:** If there is not a piece long enough to extend from corner to corner, use shorter pieces, and then place flowers over the areas where they join.

7. Stitch ¼" from the raw edges of the vine. Turn the folded edge over the stitching line,

Fig. 14

Bethlehem Star by Laura Nownes

and then stitch the folded edge to the background, either by hand or machine.

8. Use your preferred method of appliqué to prepare and then sew the flowers (L) and flower centers (M), leaves (N), and berries (O) to the background.

9. To complete the quilt top, straighten the outer edges, if necessary.

Quilting and Finishing

(See General Instructions pages 137-141)

1. Layer and baste together the quilt top, batting, and backing in preparation for quilting.

2. Hand or machine quilt. For this quilt, the large center star is quilted in the ditch; the background has a meandering stitch; the vines and flowers have outline stitches; and the Drunkard's Path is stitched following the curves of the path.

3. Finish the quilt by cutting and piecing 2¼" strips of straight-grain binding fabric. Sew binding around quilt using folded mitered corners. ❖

Lisa Stone

About sixteen years ago during a visit to Wisconsin, I watched my friend Sandy Retler work on a Log Cabin quilt. She made it look so easy that I thought I would attempt it myself when I returned home. Now, over seventy-five quilts later, I still enjoy making them, but even more, I take pleasure in giving family and friends quilts I have designed and made especially for them. My favorite types of quilts to make are appliqué. I am from the Mary Lou Weidman school of appliqué—glue is a four letter word and freezer paper rules! She taught me the importance of story quilts and to add humor and whimsy to my quilts. She has also taught me the importance of value—it can make or break a quilt. My most favorite quilts are the old ones. Those quilters didn't have any of the valuable tools we have today but still produced beautiful quilts.

I am the only quilter in our family, but my niece, Kirsten Barringer, is trying! I am so lucky because my husband, Dale, is very encouraging and gives me helpful advice, as does my sister, Gayle Lindfield.

I belong to the Amador Valley Quilt Guild, and like a lot of other quilters, I enjoy gardening, cooking, and shopping—especially fabric shopping! I started teaching quilt classes in a small store in Livermore in the late 1980s and now enjoy teaching at ThimbleCreek. I feel so very blessed to be a part of ThimbleCreek, and Roxie and Joe are very supportive of all their employees. My co-workers are a joy to work with and are also a very creative group. Look for Lisa's original patterns packaged by her company Quilt Bug Patterns.

Robot Man

Designed, made, and quilted by Lisa Stone
Finished size: 40" x 54½"

This is a great quilt for your little robot collector! The inspiration for it came from the background fabric. It reminded me of old science fiction and monster movies. Maybe your little ones have dreams of being an astronaut and visiting the robot planet! Let your children or young friends help sew on the buttons to make their "outer space" dreams come true.

Materials

Yardage (based on 42" fabric, from selvage to selvage)

Fabric 1: 2⅞ yds.* robot print
Fabric 2: ⅜ yd. dusty pink
Fabric 3: ¼ yd. tan stripe; buy ⅜ yds. if directional
Fabric 4: ⅛ yd. gray
Fabric 5: ⅛ yd. peach
Fabric 6: ¾ yd. medium tan
Fabric 7: ⅓ yd. red
Fabric 8: ½ yd. light tan
Batting: 45" x 60"
Backing: 2½ yds.
Black embroidery floss
Assorted buttons or other embellishments

** This quilt uses Fabric 1 for the binding. If you use a different fabric for the binding, deduct ⅝ yd. from Fabric 1. The total yardage for binding should be ⅝ yd.*

Cutting

(See Quilt Layout Diagram)
Cut all fabric crosswise, from selvage to selvage, unless otherwise instructed.

Star Block

(Fig. 1)

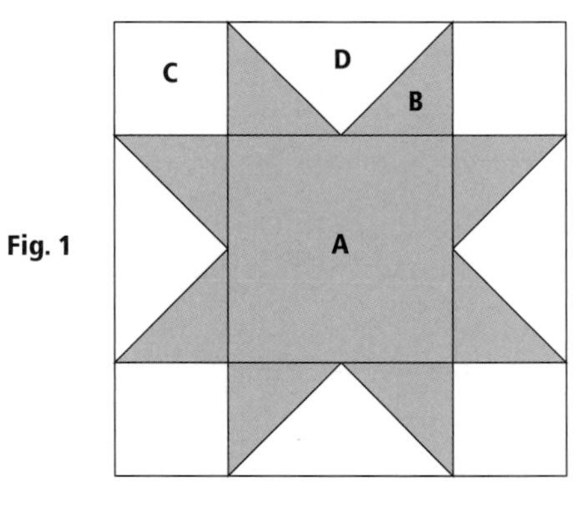

Fig. 1

FABRIC 2
Piece A: Cut six 3½" squares.
Piece B: Cut (48) 2" squares.

FABRIC 8
Piece C: Cut (24) 2" squares.
Piece D: Cut two 2" strips. Cut these strips into (24) 2" x 3½" rectangles.

Spaceship Blocks

(Fig. 2)

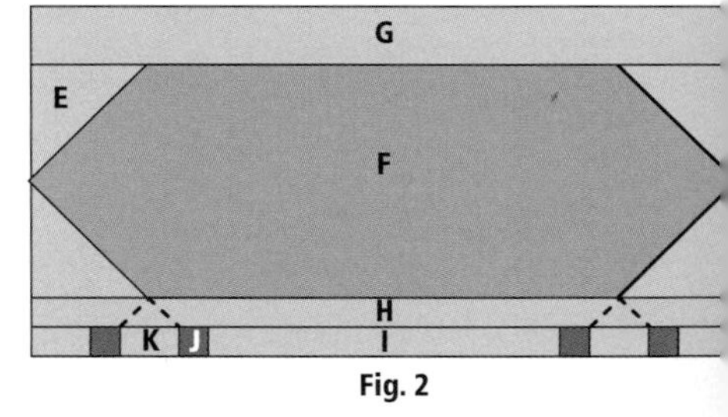

Fig. 2

FABRIC 1
Piece E: Cut (12) 2½" squares.
Piece G: Cut three 1½" x 12½" strips.
Piece H: Cut three 1" x 12½" strips.
Piece I: Cut three 1" x 6½" strips.
Piece K: Cut (12) 1" x 1½" pieces.

FABRIC 3
Piece F: Cut three 4½" x 12½" pieces.

FABRIC 4
Piece J: Cut twelve 1" squares.

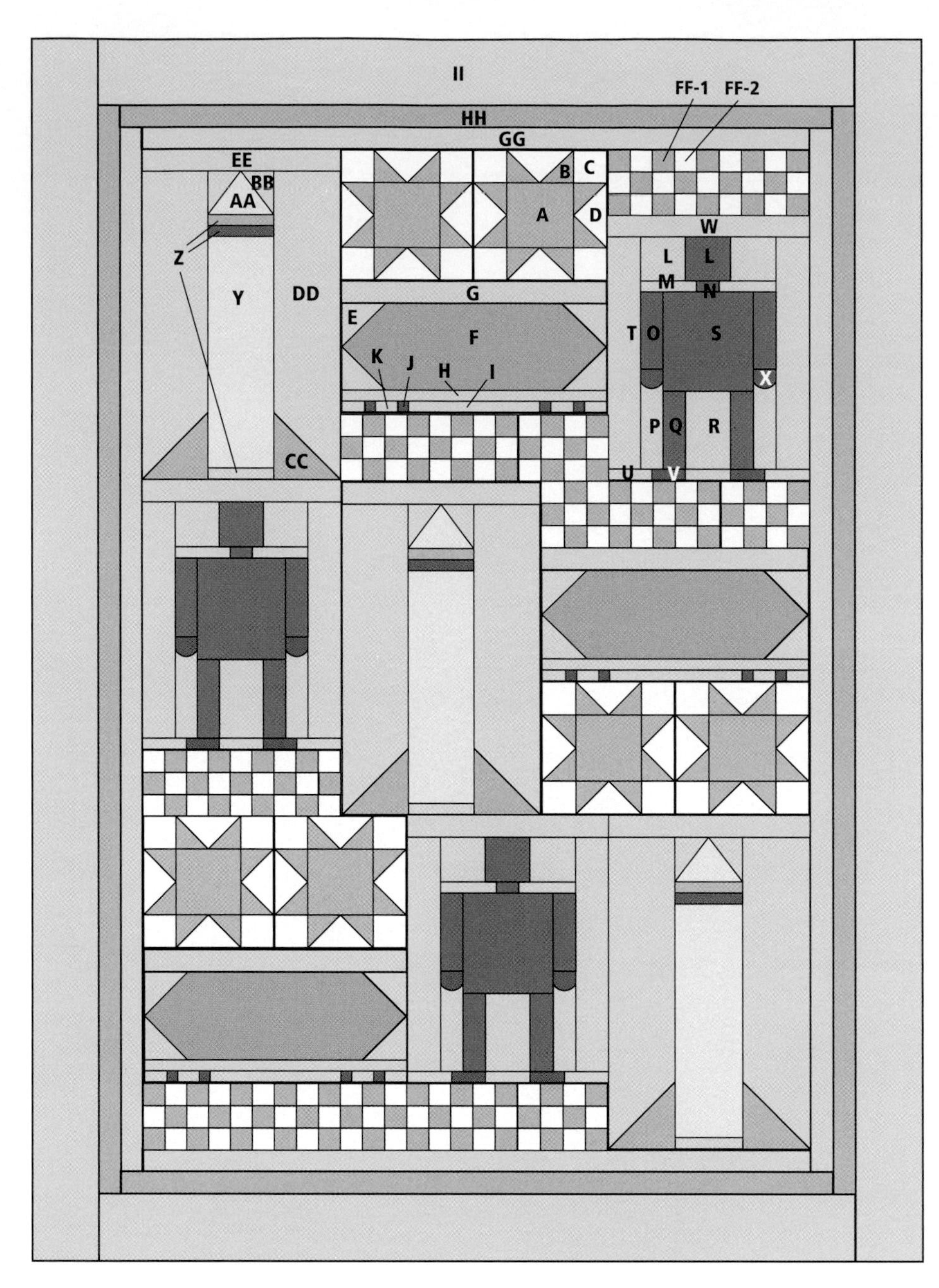

Robot Man Quilt Layout

Fabric 1 - robot print	Fabric 5 - peach
Fabric 2 - dusty pink	Fabric 6 - medium tan
Fabric 3 - tan stripe	Fabric 7 - red
Fabric 4 - gray	Fabric 8 - light tan

Robot Block

(Fig. 3.)

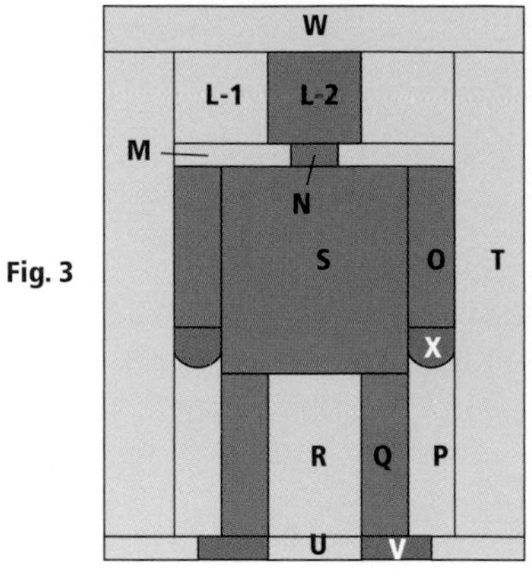

FABRIC 1

Piece L-1: Cut six 2½" squares.
Piece M: Cut six 1" x 3" strips.
Piece P: Cut six 1½" x 5" strips.
Piece R: Cut three 2½" x 4" strips.
Piece T: Cut six 2" x 11" strips.
Piece U: Cut nine 1" x 2½" strips.
Piece W: Cut three 1½" x 9½" strips.

FABRIC 7

Piece L-2: Cut three 2½" squares.
Piece N: Cut three 1" x 1½" strips.
Piece O: Cut six 1½" x 4" strips.
Piece Q: Cut six 1½" x 4" strips.
Piece S: Cut three 4½" x 5" pieces.

FABRIC 4

Piece V: Cut six 1" x 2" pieces.
Piece X: Make a template from pattern X (see General Instructions, page 132). Use Template X to cut (12) "hands."

Rocket Blocks

(Fig. 4)

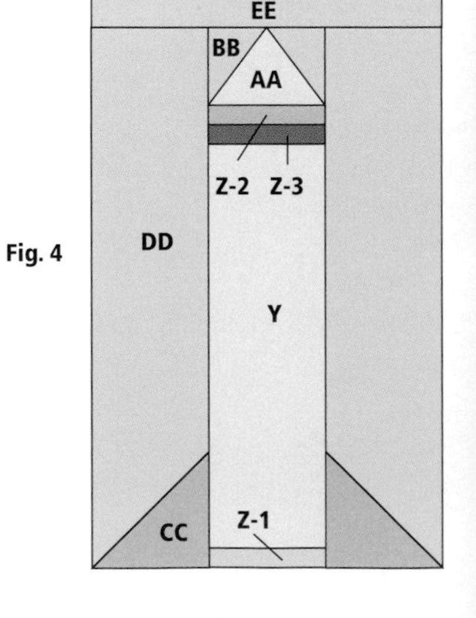

FABRIC 5

PIECE Y: Cut three 3½" x 10½" rectangles.

PIECE AA: Make a template from pattern AA. Use Template AA to cut three nose cones.

FABRIC 1

PIECE Z-1: Cut three 1" x 3½" pieces.

PIECE BB: Make a template from pattern BB. Use Template BB to cut six pieces.

PIECE EE: Cut three 1½" x 9½" strips.

PIECE DD: Cut six strips 3½" x 14½".

FABRIC 6

PIECE CC: Cut six 3½" squares.

FABRIC 2

PIECE Z-2: Cut three 1" x 3½" pieces.

FABRIC 4

PIECE Z-3: Cut three 1" x 3½" pieces.

Nine-patch Blocks

(Fig. 5)

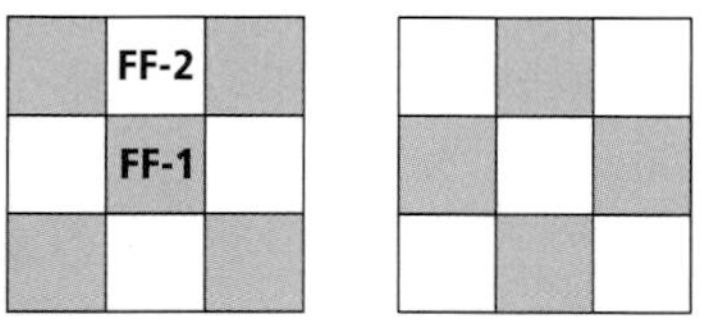

Fig. 5

FABRIC 6

PIECE FF-1: Cut six 1½" strips.

FABRIC 8

PIECE FF-2: Cut four 1½" strips.

Robot Man by Lisa Stone

Borders and Binding

(See Quilt Layout Diagram)

FABRIC 1

PIECE GG: Cut five 1½" strips for the border (GG).

PIECE II: Cut five 3½" strips for the border (II).

BINDING: Cut eight 2½" strips.

FABRIC 6

PIECE HH: Cut five 1½" strips for the border (HH).

Construction

Sew ¼" seams with right sides together unless otherwise noted.

Star Block

Finished size: 6" x 6"

(Make 6 blocks. See Fig. 2.)

To make each star block:

1. Draw a diagonal pencil line on the wrong side of all Star Block squares (B). Place one square (B) over the left corner of one rectangle (D) (Fig. 6). Sew on pencil line. Trim the seam allowance to ¼" (Fig. 6). Repeat this process for all four rectangles (D).

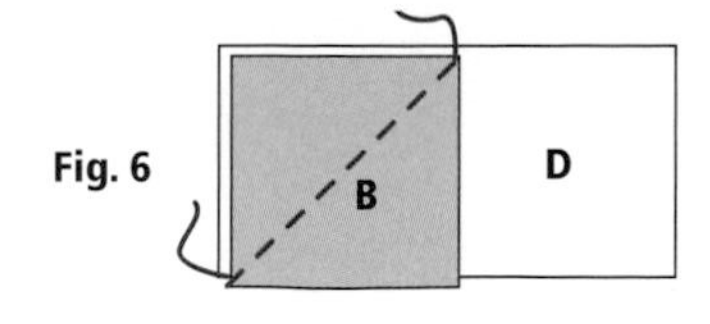

Fig. 6

2. Place another square (B) on the right corner of (B/D) unit (Fig. 7) and proceed as in Step 1. Repeat this process for all four rectangles.
3. Press back corner (B) flaps; trim points.

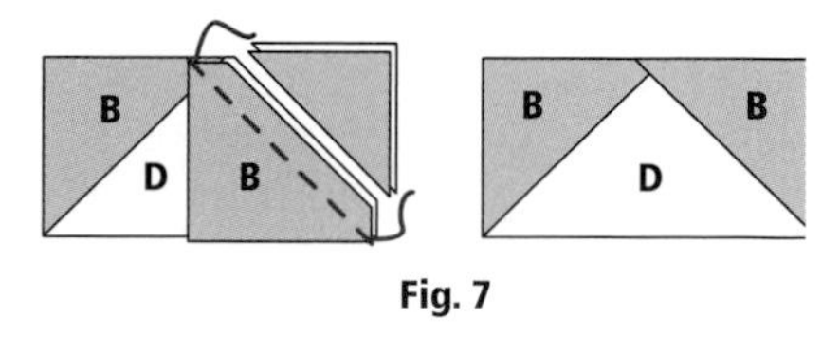

Fig. 7

4. To create the top of the block, sew a corner square (C) to both ends of a star point unit (Fig. 8, Row 1); press in direction of arrows.

5. Repeat this step for the bottom of the block.

6. Sew the two remaining star point units to opposite sides of the center square (A).

7. Sew the tops and bottom units to the center, and then press the entire block (Fig. 8).

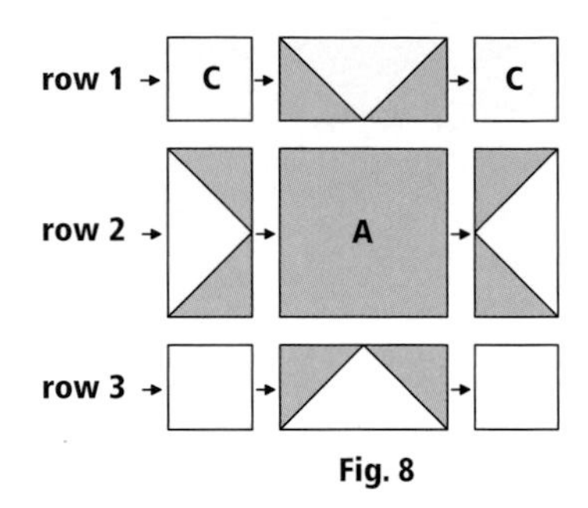

Fig. 8

Spaceship Block

Finished size: 6" x 12"

(Make 3 blocks. See Fig. 3.)

To make each spaceship block:

8. Lay out all pieces before sewing.

9. Draw a diagonal pencil line on the wrong side of all squares (E). Lay one background square (E), face down, over each corner of the spaceship (F) and sew each square on the diagonal. Trim seam allowance to ¼", and trim points. Then, fold and press each flap toward the corner (Fig. 9).

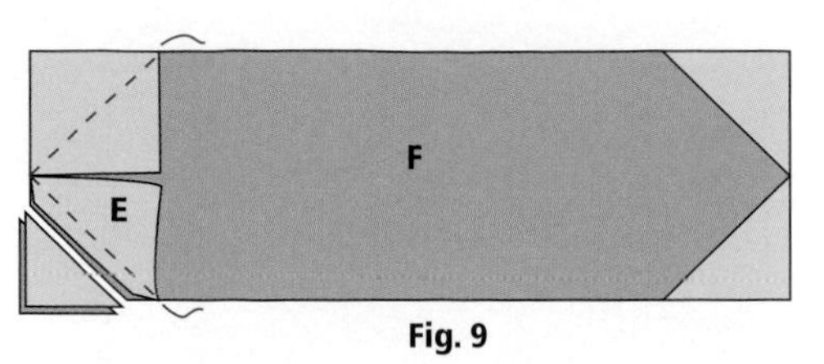

Fig. 9

10. Sew the 1½" x 12½" strip (G) to the top of the spaceship.

11. Sew the 1" x 12½" strip (H) to the bottom of the spaceship.

12. To create the spaceship's "feet," sew one background piece (K) to the left side of one square (J); press seams toward (J). Repeat this step three times for a total of four (J/K) units. Then sew one of the (J/K) units to another pair; repeat this step.

13. Sew the finished feet to the sides of the 1" x 6½" strip (I) and press seams toward I (Fig. 10).

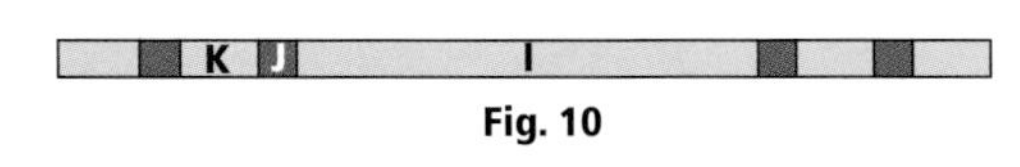

Fig. 10

14. Sew the finished strip to the 1" x 12½" strip (H) on the bottom of the spaceship; press seams (E).

15. Run a stem stitch (Fig. 11) between the spaceship and the feet (see Fig. 2—for placement).

Robot Block

Finished size: 9" x 12".

(Make 3 blocks. See Fig. 3.)

To make each robot block:

16. Lay out all pieces before sewing, referring to Fig. 12. Press seams in direction of arrows.

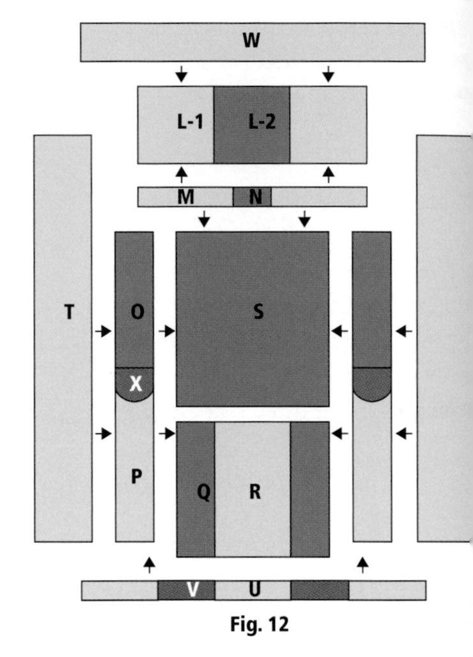

Fig. 12

17. Sew the sides (L-1) to each side of the head (L-2) (Fig. 13).

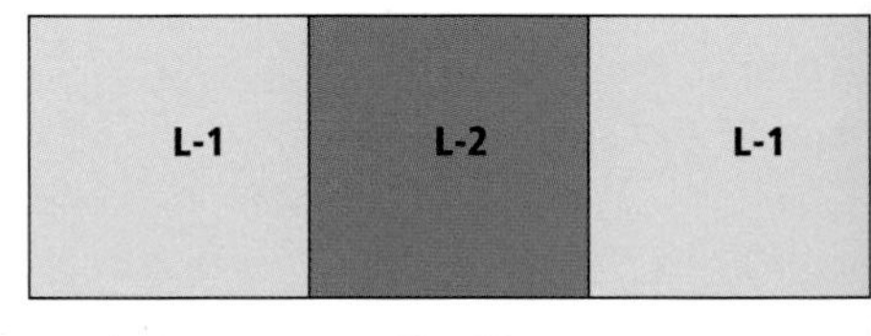

Fig. 13

18. Sew the sides (M) to each side of the neck (N).

19. Sew the hands (X), right sides together, and then turn inside out; clip, trim, and press.

20. Sew the hands to the arms (O). Sew the

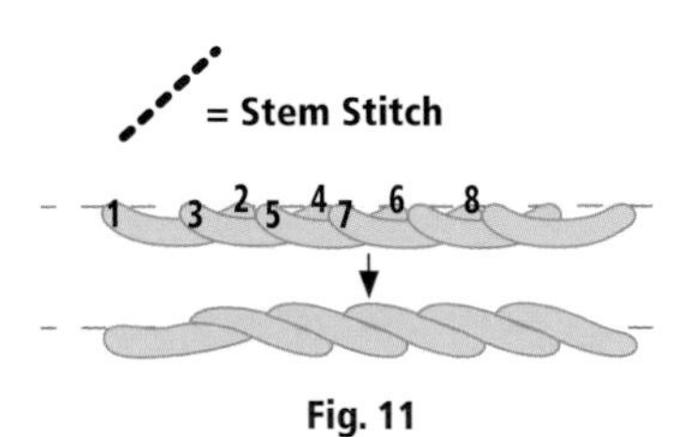

Fig. 11

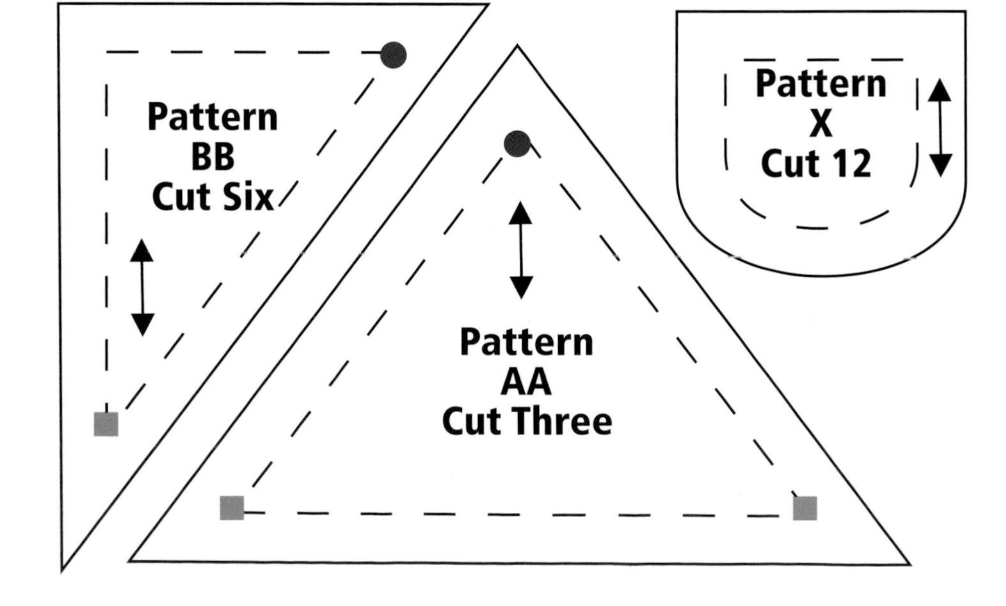

arm units to the background strips (P), and then press to flatten, if necessary.

21. Sew the legs (Q) to each side of the background (R).

22. Sew the leg unit to the torso (S).

23. Sew the arm units to the torso unit.

24. Sew the neck units to the head units, and then sew these pieces to the torso unit.

25. Sew the boots (V) to each background piece (U), and then sew this unit to the bottom of the leg unit, lining up the boots and legs.

26. Sew the background strips (T) to the sides of the finished unit, and then sew the background strip (W) to the top.

Rocket

Finished size: 9" x 15"
(Make 3 blocks. See Fig. 4.)

27. Draw a diagonal pencil line on the wrong side of all squares (CC). Lay out all pieces before sewing.

28. To create each fin, lay one 3½" square (CC), face down, over the bottom of one of the 3½" x 14½" side strips (DD), and then sew each square on the diagonal. Trim seam allowance to ¼". Then, fold and press each flap away from the strip, and trim points (Fig. 14).

29. Sew the 1" x 3½" background strip (Z-1) to the "bottom" of the rocket body (Y); press toward Y.

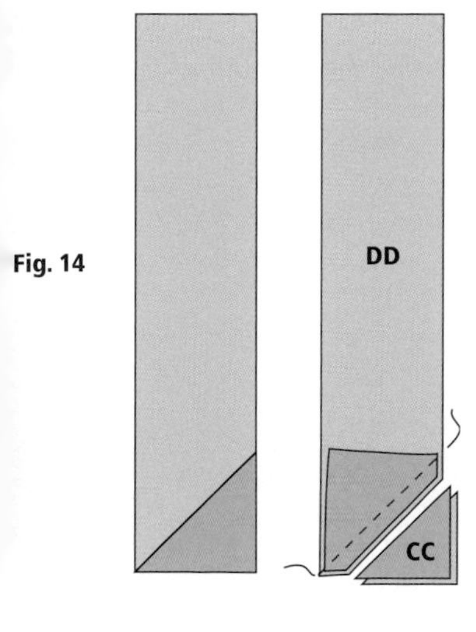

Fig. 14

30. Sew together the two remaining strips (Z-2 and Z-3). Then, sew the unit to the rocket body unit; press toward (BB).

31. Sew the background pieces (BB) to each side of the nose cone (AA).

32. Sew the nose cone unit to the top of the rocket unit; press toward rocket unit.

33. Sew the side units (CC/DD) to the rocket unit; press toward side unit.

34. Sew the 1½" x 9½" strip (EE) to the top of the unit. Press toward (EE).

Nine-Patch

Finished size: 3" x 3"
(Fig. 5)

For each nine-patch block:

35. Sew a dark strip (FF-1) to both sides of a light strip (FF-2). Press the seams toward the dark strip. Cut this unit into 1½" x 3½" pieces (Fig. 15).

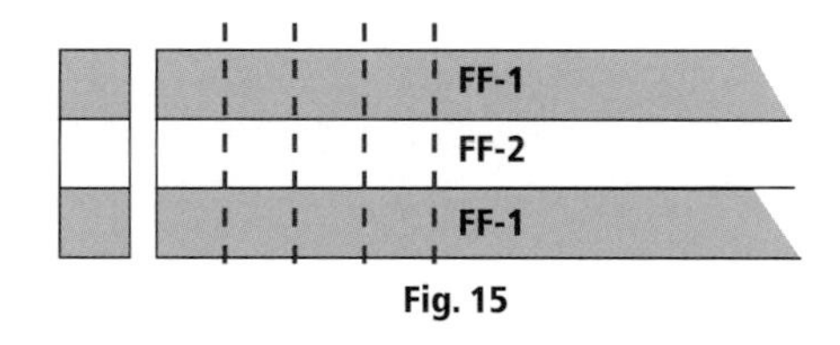

Fig. 15

36. Sew a light strip (FF) to both sides of a dark strip (FF). Press the seams toward the dark strip. Cut this unit into 1½" x 3½" pieces.

37. Make either a light or dark nine-patch block by sewing together 3 rows of alternating dark and light, and light and dark FF units as shown in Fig. 16. You will need to make a total of 11 dark nine-patch blocks, and 10 light nine-patch blocks.

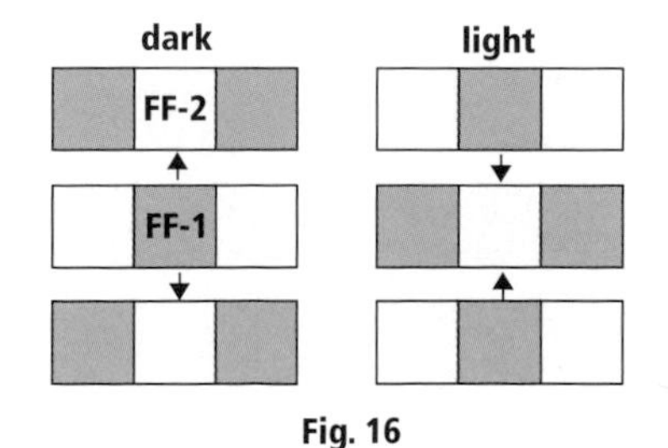

Fig. 16

Assembly

(Fig. 17)
Press all seams in any direction unless otherwise noted.

Row 1

1. Sew together two star blocks, and then sew them to the top of a spaceship block; press.

2. Sew together four nine-patch blocks, starting with a light block, and then sew these units to the bottom of the spaceship block.

3. Sew three nine-patch blocks together, starting with a dark block, and then sew these units to the top of a robot block.

4. Sew the rocket unit to the spaceship unit; press toward rocket units. Then sew these units to the robot unit.

Row 2

5. Sew together three nine-patch blocks, starting with a light block, and then sew these units to the bottom of a robot block.

6. Sew the robot unit to a rocket block; press seam toward rocket block.

7. Sew together four nine-patch blocks, starting with a light block, and then sew this unit to the top of a spaceship block.

8. Sew together two stars, and then sew them to the bottom of a spaceship block. Attach this unit to the rocket unit.

Row 3

9. Sew together two star blocks, and then sew them to the top of a spaceship block.

10. Sew together four nine-patch blocks, starting with a dark block, and then sew this unit to the bottom of the spaceship.

11. Sew together three nine-patch blocks, starting with a light block, and then sew this unit to the bottom of a robot block.

12. Sew the spaceship unit to the robot unit, and then sew these units to a rocket block.

Final Assembly

(Fig. 18)

(Press all seams.)

13. Sew the three rows to one another.

14. To create the first border, measure the top and bottom of your quilt. Trim two 1½" strips of background fabric (GG) to this length, and then sew them to the quilt. Measure the sides of your quilt. Trim (and piece, if necessary) two 1½" strips (GG) to this length. Sew them to the sides of the quilt.

15. To create the second border, repeat Step 14 using 1½" strips (HH), except measure down center of quilt including borders.

16. To create the outside border, repeat Step 14 and 15 using 3½" strips (II).

Quilting and Finishing

(See General Instructions pages 137–141)

1. Layer and baste together the quilt top, batting, and backing in preparation for quilting.

2. Hand or machine quilt. I machine quilted using blue thread and a wavy motion to make it look like the robots and spaceships are lifting off. I added a square ¼" in from center of the star block, straight vertical lines in nine-patch blocks and a horizontal line across the center of the space ship.

3. Sew together the binding strips, and then finish the quilt by sewing the binding around the edges of the quilt.

4. Add buttons or other embellishments to complete your quilt.

5. Finish the quilt by piecing 2¼" strips of straight-grain binding fabric. Sew binding around quilt using folded mitered corners.❖

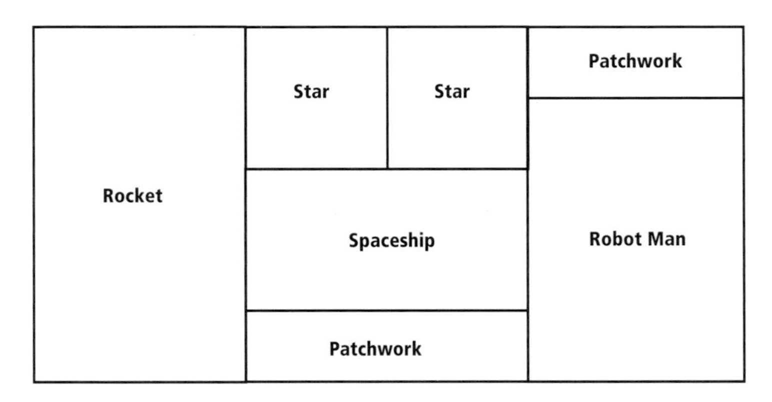

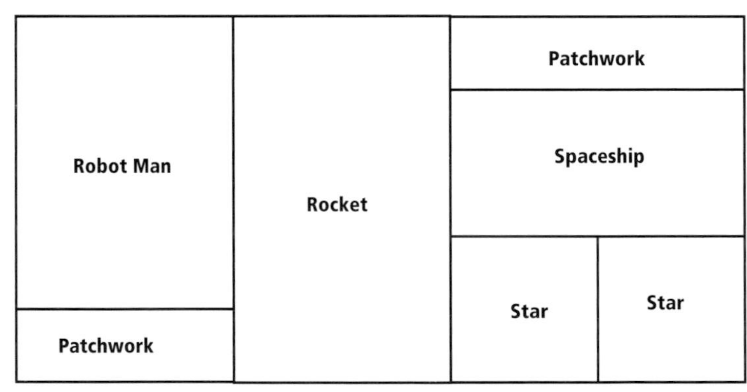

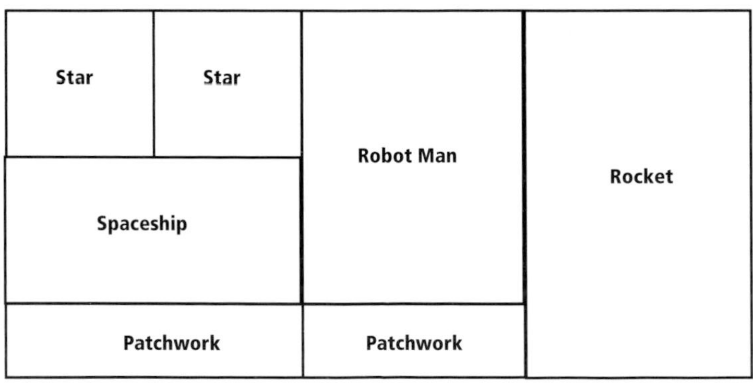

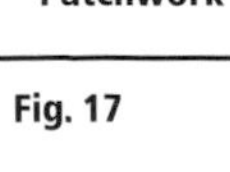

Fig. 17

Fig. 18

Roxie Wood

By hosting holiday boutiques in my home I was able to be a stay-at-home mom. My Snow Goose Boutique was very successful for ten years. I met many great people and thoroughly enjoyed that experience. My love of crafts evolved into a love of quilting. I began to work part-time at a local quilt shop. Soon I was teaching classes and totally hooked. The natural evolution was ThimbleCreek.

I am content when surrounded by fabric. Inspiration comes from many sources: fabrics, patterns, books, the great outdoors, etc. I'm a collector of fabric—an addiction to be sure (but a good addiction!). I love traditional fabrics such as plaids, stripes, civil war prints, and 1930s reproductions. I try to incorporate my fabric stash into new projects, combining older fabrics with new.

I always have many projects in various stages going at the same time. I also participate in group exchanges with shop employees or with our quilt group, Lavender Bags. Group exchanges are great; I end up with something unique every time.

Family and quilting are very important to me. I love working with Joe. Our customers are delightful and the staff is extraordinary. I wake up with a smile because I get to go to work. Quilting allows me to create heirlooms for my family. And I can't wait to have grandchildren. Imagine the excitement of passing on to another generation the thrill of quilting!

Dancing Pinwheels

Designed and made by Roxie Wood; quilted by Ginger Hayes
Finished size: 75" x 91"

I've always wanted to make this quilt. I've had it on my drawing board for quite some time. I love 1930s reproductions, and this quilt design lent itself perfectly to these patterns and colors. I wanted the quilt to be happy and sunny, so I chose solid yellow to complement the 1930s cheery color scheme. You could also use batiks or solids, or go totally scrappy. I hope you enjoy making this quilt as much as I did. There is lots of strip cutting to help save you time.

Materials

Yardage (based on 42" fabric, from selvage to selvage)

Fabric 1: 5¾ yds. white
Fabric 2: 3½ yds. yellow
Fabric 3: ⅜ yd. each of 16 assorted 1930s fabrics
Backing: 5 yds.
Binding: ½ yd.
Batting: 81" x 96" or queen size

Cutting Instructions

(See Quilt Layout Diagram)
Cut all fabric crosswise, from selvage to selvage, unless otherwise instructed.

FABRIC 1

Piece A: Cut five 6⅞" strips. Cut each strip into 6⅞" squares, and then cut each square on the diagonal to create 60 triangles.

Piece C: Cut (46) 2⅜" strips. Cut each strip into 2⅜" squares, and then cut each square on the diagonal to create 1,532 triangles.

Piece F: Cut five 5½" strips. Cut each strip into 5½" squares, and then cut each square on both diagonals to create 132 setting triangles for the pinwheel border.

Piece G: Cut two 3½" strips. Cut each strip into 3½" squares, and then cut each square on the diagonal to create 16 corner triangles for the pinwheel border.

FABRIC 2

Piece I: Cut four 1¾" strips by the length of the fabric for the outer border.
Piece B: Cut ten 6⅞" x 26" strips. Cut each strip into 6⅞" squares, and then cut each square on the diagonal to create 60 triangles.
Piece E: Cut (15) 2⅜" x 26" strips. Cut each strip into 2⅜" squares, and then cut each square on the diagonal to create 300 triangles (set aside 16 triangles for pinwheel border corners).

FABRIC 3

Piece D: From each of the 16 fabrics, cut two 2⅜" strips and one 2⅜" x 21" strip. Cut each strip into 2⅜" squares, and then cut each square on the diagonal to create 80 triangles per fabric (1,280 total).

Floating Pinwheels

Designed and made by Joe Wood; quilted by Lynne Todoroff
Finished size: 52" x 68"

For this quilt, I used a simple pinwheel design to help showcase the suede-like nuances of hand-dyed fabric. The neutral, complementary fabrics for the alternate blocks and sashing create the impression that the pinwheels are "floating" in space. Depending on the look you want, this quilt can be made entirely scrappy or with a more selective assortment of fabrics. Either way, it's important when creating the pinwheels to choose color combinations that work well together. If you want single-colored pinwheels, select your fabric sets before beginning the pinwheel construction. For the most part, I paired light and dark fabrics. To add a little variety, I occasionally paired dark and dark fabrics.

Materials

Yardage (based on 42" fabric, from selvage to selvage)

Fabric 1: ¼ yd. each of 6 assorted light hand-dyed fabrics
Fabric 2: ¼ yd. each of 6 assorted dark hand-dyed fabrics
Fabric 3: 1 yd. small brown plaid
Fabric 4: 2 yds. medium brown plaid
Backing: 4 yds.
Binding: ⅝ yd.
Batting: 72" x 80" or twin size

Cutting

(See Quilt Layout Diagram)
Cut all fabric crosswise, from selvage to selvage, unless otherwise instructed.

Pinwheel Blocks

(Fig. 1)

Fig. 1

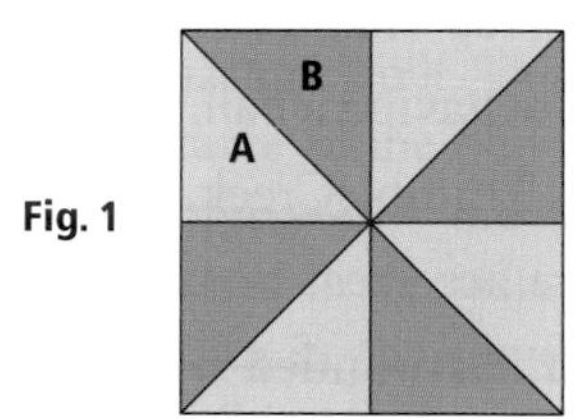

FABRIC 1

Piece A: From each light hand-dyed fabric cut (20) 2⅞" squares, and then cut each square on the diagonal to create a total of 240 triangles.

FABRIC 2

Piece B: From each dark hand-dyed fabric cut (20) 2⅞" squares, and then cut each square on the diagonal to create a total of 240 triangles.

3. To make ironing easier, remove fabrics from dryer while they are slightly damp. Refold each fabric lengthwise (as it was on the bolt) with wrong sides together and matching selvages. If necessary, adjust slightly at selvages so that fold lays flat. Press each fabric using a steam iron set on "Cotton."

CUTTING FABRIC

Fabrics have two grain lines: a straight-grain, which runs along the length of the fabric (warp) and a cross-grain that runs along the width of the fabric (weft). The exact diagonal between these two is the true bias. Your choice of grain line will depend on how you want the fabric to act. Pieces cut on the straight-grain will have the maximum strength and minimum amount of "give." Pieces cut on the cross-grain will have moderate strength and stability. Pieces cut on the bias will have maximum flexibility and very little stability and strength. An easy way to find the grain lines is to pull one thread from the width. Fabric on either side of the thread will pucker, allowing you to trim the raw edge.

Strip quilting starts on the cutting board. In strip quilting, a strip of fabric is cut to the length common to several pieces by the width of the fabric. Once you have a true cross-grain, cut all strips from the selvage-to-selvage width of the fabric unless otherwise indicated. Trim off the selvages.

"Fussy-cutting" is the term for another method favored by some of the designers in this book. By choosing to cut your basic block from a repeated printed element of the purchased fabric, you can add interest and complexity.

Use sticky notes to label cut fabric pieces with their piece "letters." This will speed construction.

Rotary Cutting

Rotary cutting has brought speed and accuracy to quiltmaking. Rotary cutters are extremely sharp, so be sure to read the product instructions carefully and observe the safety precautions. Choose one that is comfortable to hold. With a smooth downward motion, run the blade of the rotary cutter firmly along the right edge of the ruler. Always cut in a direction away from your body and develop a habit of closing the blade guard immediately after cutting.

1. Follow **Preparing Fabrics**, page 129, to wash, dry, and press fabrics.
2. Cut all strips from the selvage-to-selvage width of the fabric unless otherwise indicated in project instructions. Place fabric on the cutting mat, as shown in Fig. 1, with the fold of the fabric toward you. To straighten the uneven fabric edge, make the first "squaring up" cut by placing the right edge of the rotary cutting ruler over the left raw edge of the fabric. Place right-angle triangle (or another rotary cutting ruler) with the lower edge carefully aligned with the fold and the left edge against the ruler (Fig. 1). Hold the ruler firmly with your left hand,

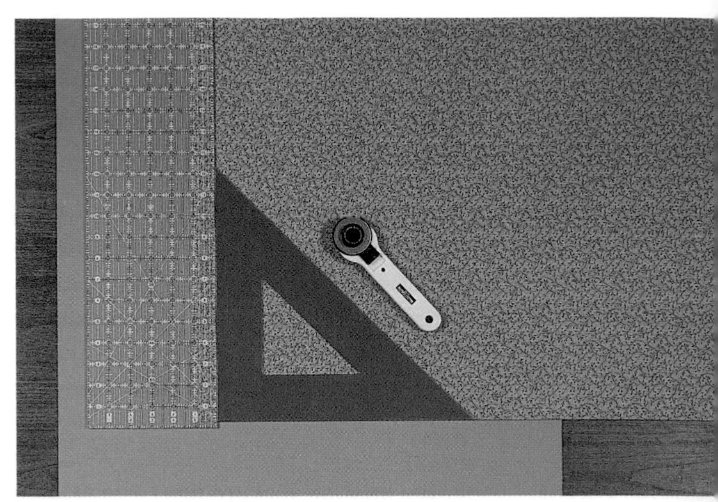

Fig. 1

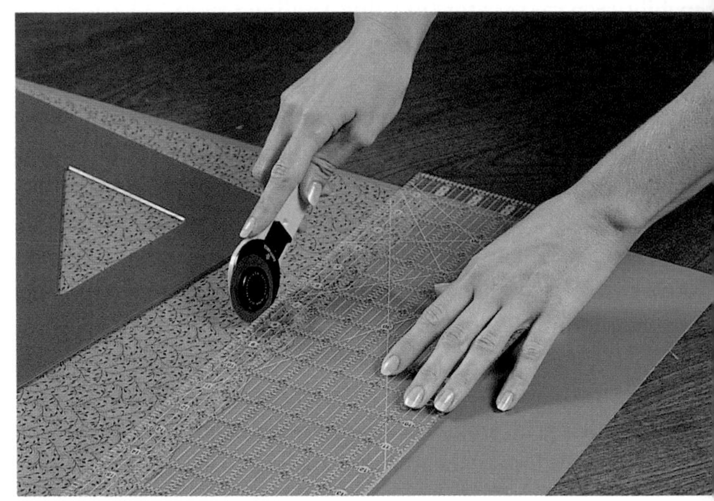

Fig. 2

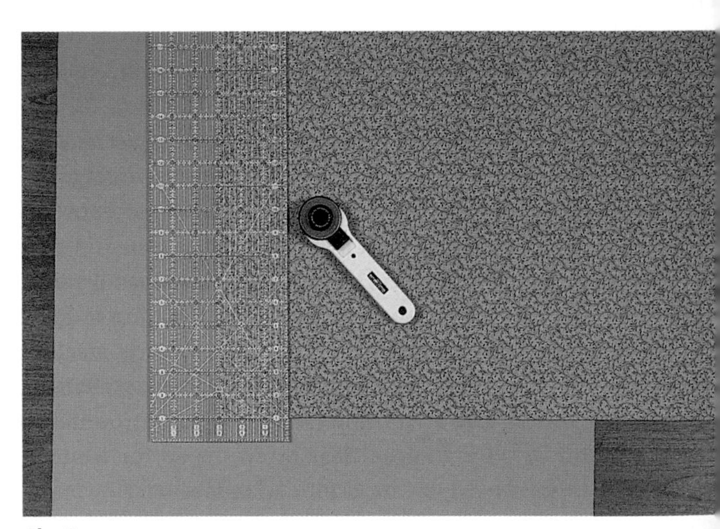

Fig. 3

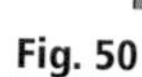

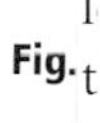

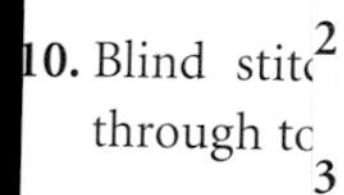

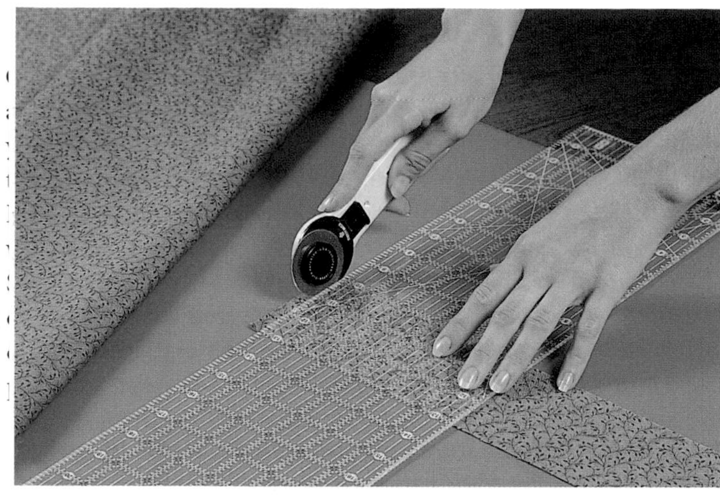

Fig. 4

Fig. 5

Fig. 6

Fig. 7

placing your little finger off the left edge to anchor the ruler. Remove the triangle, pick up the rotary cutter, and retract the blade guard. Using a smooth downward motion, make the cut by running the blade of the rotary cutter firmly along the right edge of the ruler (Fig. 2). Always cut in a direction away from your body and immediately close the blade guard after each cut.

3. To cut each of the strips required for a project, place the ruler over the cut edge of the fabric, aligning desired marking on the ruler with the cut edge (Fig. 3); make the cut. When cutting several strips from a single piece of fabric, it is important to occasionally use the ruler and triangle to ensure that cuts are still at a perfect right angle to the fold. If not, repeat Step 2 to straighten.
4. To square up selvage ends of a strip before cutting pieces, refer to Fig. 4 and place folded strip on mat with selvage ends to your right. Aligning a horizontal marking on ruler with 1 long edge of strip, use rotary cutter to trim selvage to make end of strip square and even (Fig. 4). Turn strip (or entire mat) so that cut end is to your left before making subsequent cuts.
5. Pieces such as rectangles and squares can now be cut from strips. (Cutting other shapes such as diamonds is discussed in individual project instructions.) Usually strips remain folded, and pieces are cut in pairs after ends of strips are squared up. To cut squares or rectangles from a strip, place ruler over left end of strip, aligning desired marking on ruler with cut end of strip. To ensure perfectly square cuts, align a horizontal marking on ruler with 1 long edge of strip (Fig. 5) before making the cut.
6. To cut 2 triangles from a square, cut square the size indicated in the project instructions. Cut square once diagonally to make 2 triangles (Fig. 6).
7. To cut 4 triangles from a square, cut square the size indicated in the project instructions. Cut square twice diagonally to make 4 triangles (Fig. 7). You may find it helpful to use a small rotary cutting mat so that the mat can be turned to make second cut without disturbing fabric pieces.
8. After some practice, you may want to try stacking up to 6 fabric layers when making cuts. When stacking strips, match long cut edges and follow Step 4 to square up ends of strip stack. Carefully turn stack (or entire mat) so that squared-up ends are to your left before making subsequent cuts. After cutting check accuracy of pieces. Some shapes, such as diamonds, are more difficult to cut accurately in stacks.

Index